W9-CHE-872

pasta

...made simple

This edition published in 2011
LOVE FOOD is an imprint of Parragon Books Ltd

Parragon
Queen Street House
4 Queen Street
Bath BA1 1HE, UK

ISBN: 978-1-4454-3057-7

Printed in China

Produced by Ivy Contract
Photography by Charlie Paul

Notes for the Reader

This book uses imperial, metric, and US cup measurements. Follow the same units of measurement throughout; do not mix imperial and metric. All spoon measurements are level: teaspoons are assumed to be 5 ml, and tablespoons are assumed to be 15 ml. Unless otherwise stated, milk is assumed to be whole, eggs and individual vegetables, such as potatoes, are medium, and pepper is freshly ground black pepper.

The times given are an approximate guide only. Preparation times differ according to the techniques used by different people and the cooking times may also vary from those given as a result of the type of oven used. Optional ingredients, variations, or serving suggestions have not been included in the calculations.

Recipes using raw or very lightly cooked eggs should be avoided by infants, the elderly, pregnant women, convalescents, and anyone with a chronic condition. Pregnant and breast-feeding women are advised to avoid eating peanuts and peanut products. People with nut allergies should be aware that some of the prepared ingredients used in the recipes in this book may contain nuts. Always check the package before use.

Vegetarians should be aware that some of the prepared ingredients used in the recipes in this book may contain animal products. Always check the package before use.

pasta

introduction

Where would we be without pasta? It has to be the most useful invention ever—it is delicious, inexpensive, nutritious, quick and easy to cook, very satisfying, and incredibly versatile. The fact that it comes in so many shapes and sizes makes it even more interesting, as well as fun to eat for adults and children alike.

The shape you use is largely a matter of choice, and you have about 200 different shapes to choose from! There are, of course, a few classic combinations. Spaghetti, for example, is the one to serve with meatballs or a rich, meaty, bolognese sauce—if you want to be both well fed and entertained, look out for the really long variety of spaghetti, which is quite a challenge to eat! Macaroni & Cheese simply wouldn't be the same made with any other shape of pasta, and Fettuccine Alfredo has a ring to the name that pasta lovers know well!

Pasta is almost foolproof to cook, but it's worth noting one or two points. Firstly, always bring the cooking water to a rapid boil before adding the pasta. Once the pasta is in the pan, adjust the heat so that the pasta cooks at a steady boil without boiling over. An important thing to remember is not to overcook the pasta. 'Al dente' means 'still firm when bitten' and this is what you need to aim for—eating limp, soggy pasta is quite an unpleasant experience. Follow the recommended cooking time in the recipe or on the package and keep tasting toward the end of the time to make sure you get it just right—or you can, of course, follow the Italian tradition of throwing a test piece at the wall and if it sticks, you'll know it's done!

Making your own fresh pasta is surprisingly easy and there are a few recipes for you to try. For everyday use, though, fill your store cupboards with a good variety of pasta shapes, select your favorite dishes, and make the most of this treasure of an ingredient.

soups & salads

minestrone soup

ingredients

serves 6

2 tbsp olive oil
2 oz/55 g rindless pancetta or lean bacon, diced
2 onions, sliced
2 garlic cloves, finely chopped
3 carrots, chopped
2 celery stalks, chopped
8 oz/225 g/1 cup dried cannellini beans, soaked overnight in cold water to cover
14 oz/400 g canned chopped tomatoes
64 fl oz/2 liters/8 cups beef stock
12 oz/350 g potatoes, diced
6 oz/175 g dried pepe bucato, macaroni, or other soup pasta shapes
6 oz/175 g green beans, sliced
4 oz/115 g/1 cup fresh or frozen peas
8 oz/225 g savoy cabbage, shredded
3 tbsp chopped fresh flat-leaf parsley
salt and pepper
fresh Parmesan cheese shavings, to serve

method

1 Heat the olive oil in a large, heavy-bottom pan. Add the pancetta, onions, and garlic and cook, stirring occasionally, for 5 minutes.

2 Add the carrots and celery and cook, stirring occasionally, for an additional 5 minutes, or until all the vegetables are softened.

3 Drain the soaked beans and add them to the pan with the tomatoes and their can juices and the beef stock. Bring to a boil, then reduce the heat, cover, and let simmer for 1 hour.

4 Add the potatoes, re-cover, and cook for 15 minutes, then add the pasta, green beans, peas, cabbage, and parsley. Cover and cook for an additional 15 minutes, or until all the vegetables are tender. Season with salt and pepper. Ladle the soup into warmed soup bowls and serve immediately with Parmesan cheese shavings.

hearty bean & pasta soup

ingredients

serves 4

4 tbsp olive oil
1 onion, finely chopped
1 celery stalk, chopped
1 carrot, peeled and diced
1 bay leaf
2 pints/1.2 liters/5 cups vegetable stock
14 oz/400 g canned chopped tomatoes
6 oz/175 g dried pasta shapes, such as farfalle, shells, or twists
14 oz/400 g canned cannellini beans, drained and rinsed
7 oz/200 g spinach or Swiss chard, thick stalks removed, and shredded
salt and pepper
1½ oz/40 g/⅓ cup finely grated Parmesan cheese, to serve

method

1. Heat the olive oil in a large heavy-bottom saucepan. Add the onion, celery, and carrot and cook over medium heat for 8–10 minutes, stirring occasionally, until the vegetables have softened. Add the bay leaf, stock, and chopped tomatoes, then bring to a boil.
2. Reduce the heat, cover, and simmer for 15 minutes, or until the vegetables are just tender. Add the pasta and beans, then bring the soup back to a boil and cook for 10 minutes, or according to the package directions, until the pasta is just tender. Stir occasionally to prevent the pasta from sticking to the bottom of the pan and burning.
3. Season to taste, add the spinach, and cook for another 2 minutes, or until tender. Serve the soup in warmed bowls, sprinkled with Parmesan cheese.

variation

Try other beans, such as pinto, black-eyed peas, or chickpeas, if you wish. Lentils, such as green lentils, also make a tasty and nutritious alternative.

tomato broth with angel-hair pasta

ingredients

serves 4

1 lb 2 oz/500 g ripe tomatoes, peeled and halved
8 garlic cloves, peeled but left whole
1 Bermuda onion, chopped
½ tsp saffron threads, lightly crushed
1 tsp sugar
1 bouquet garni
2-inch/5-cm strip thinly pared lemon rind
1 pint/600 ml/2½ cups vegetable or chicken stock
2 tbsp extra virgin olive oil
10 oz/280 g dried angel-hair pasta
salt and pepper

method

1 Put the tomatoes, garlic cloves, onion, saffron, sugar, bouquet garni, and lemon rind into a large heavy-bottom saucepan. Pour in the stock and bring to a boil, then lower the heat, cover, and simmer, stirring occasionally, for 25–30 minutes, until the tomatoes have disintegrated.

2 Remove the pan from the heat and let cool slightly. Remove and discard the garlic cloves, bouquet garni, and lemon rind. Ladle the tomato mixture into a food processor or blender and process to a puree. Return the puree to the rinsed-out pan and season to taste with salt and pepper. Stir in the oil and bring to a boil. Add the pasta, bring back to a boil, and cook for 2–4 minutes, until tender but still firm to the bite.

3 Taste and adjust the seasoning, if necessary. Ladle the broth and pasta into warmed soup bowls and serve immediately.

tortellini in broth

ingredients

serves 6

3 tbsp olive oil
1 red onion, finely chopped
2 garlic cloves, finely chopped
12 oz/350 g fresh ground beef
1 tsp finely chopped fresh thyme
1 fresh rosemary sprig, finely chopped
1 bay leaf
3 pints/1.7 liters/7 cups beef stock
basic pasta dough (see below)
all-purpose flour, for dusting
1 egg, lightly beaten
salt and pepper

basic pasta dough

7 oz/200 g white bread flour
½ tsp salt
½ tsp olive oil
1 egg, lightly beaten

method

1 Heat the oil in a saucepan. Add the onion and garlic and cook over a low heat, stirring occasionally, until softened. Add the beef, increase the heat to medium and cook for 8–10 minutes, until evenly browned.

2 Stir in the herbs, season to taste with salt and pepper, add ½ cup of the stock and bring to the boil. Cover and simmer for 25 minutes, then remove the lid and cook until all the liquid has evaporated. Remove from the heat and discard the bay leaf.

3 Make a double quantity of pasta dough, working the oil and beaten eggs into the flour and salt. Knead vigorously to form a stiff dough. Allow to rest for 30 minutes, then roll out the dough thinly on a lightly floured surface. Using a plain cookie cutter, stamp out rounds. Place the meat mixture in the centre of each round. Brush the edges with a little beaten egg, then fold them in half to make half moons and seal. Wrap these around the tip of your index finger until the corners meet and press together to seal. Place on a floured dish towel and leave to dry for 30 minutes.

4 Bring the remaining stock to the boil in a saucepan. Add the tortellini, bring back to the boil and cook until tender but still firm to the bite. Ladle the tortellini and broth into warmed soup bowls and serve immediately.

italian chicken soup

ingredients

serves 4

1 lb/450 g skinless, boneless chicken breast, cut into thin strips
40 fl oz/1.25 liters/5 cups chicken stock
5 fl oz/150 ml/⅔ cup heavy cream
4 oz/115 g dried vermicelli
1 tbsp cornstarch
3 tbsp milk
6 oz/175 g canned corn kernels, drained
salt and pepper

method

1. Place the chicken in a large pan and pour in the chicken stock and cream. Bring to a boil, then reduce the heat and let simmer for 20 minutes.

2. Meanwhile, bring a large heavy-bottom pan of lightly salted water to a boil. Add the pasta, return to a boil, and cook for 10–12 minutes, or until just tender but still firm to the bite. Drain the pasta well and keep warm.

3. Season the soup with salt and pepper. Mix the cornstarch and milk together until a smooth paste forms, then stir it into the soup. Add the corn and pasta and heat through. Ladle the soup into warmed soup bowls and serve.

fish soup with anellini

ingredients

serves 6

2 tbsp olive oil
2 onions, sliced
1 garlic clove, finely chopped
32 fl oz/1 liter/4 cups fish stock or water
14 oz/400 g canned chopped tomatoes
¼ tsp herbes de Provence
¼ tsp saffron threads
4 oz/115 g dried anellini
1 lb/450 g monkfish fillet, cut into chunks
18 live mussels, scrubbed and debearded*
8 oz/225 g raw shrimp, shelled and deveined, tails left on
salt and pepper

* discard any damaged mussels or any that do not shut immediately when tapped; once cooked, discard any mussels that remain closed

method

1 Heat the olive oil in a large heavy-bottom pan. Add the onions and garlic and cook over low heat, stirring occasionally, for 5 minutes, or until the onions have softened.

2 Add the fish stock with the tomatoes and their can juices, herbs, saffron, and pasta, and season with salt and pepper. Bring to a boil, then cover and let simmer for 15 minutes.

3 Add the fish, mussels, and shrimp. Re-cover the pan and let simmer for an additional 5–10 minutes, until the mussels have opened, the shrimp have changed color, and the fish is opaque and flakes easily. Ladle the soup into warmed bowls and serve.

white bean soup

ingredients

serves 4

- 6 oz/175 g/3/4 cup dried cannellini beans, soaked overnight in cold water to cover
- 48 fl oz/1.6 liters/6 cups chicken or vegetable stock
- 4 oz/115 g dried spirali
- 6 tbsp olive oil
- 2 garlic cloves, finely chopped
- 4 tbsp chopped fresh flat-leaf parsley
- salt and pepper
- fresh crusty bread, to serve

method

1. Drain the soaked beans and place them in a large, heavy-bottom pan. Add the stock and bring to a boil. Partially cover the pan, reduce the heat, and let simmer for 2 hours, or until tender.

2. Transfer about half the beans and a little of the stock to a food processor or blender and process to a smooth puree. Return the puree to the pan and stir well to mix. Return the soup to a boil.

3. Add the pasta to the soup, return to a boil, and cook for 10 minutes, or until tender.

4. Meanwhile, heat 4 tablespoons of the olive oil in a small pan. Add the garlic and cook over low heat, stirring frequently, for 4–5 minutes, or until golden. Stir the garlic into the soup and add the parsley. Season with salt and pepper and ladle into warmed soup bowls. Drizzle with the remaining olive oil and serve immediately with crusty bread.

vegetable & bean soup

ingredients

serves 4–6

8 oz/225 g fresh fava beans
2 tbsp olive oil
2 large garlic cloves, crushed
1 large onion, finely chopped
1 celery stalk, finely chopped
1 carrot, peeled and chopped
6 oz/175 g new potatoes, diced
30 fl oz/940 ml/3¾ cups vegetable stock
2 beefsteak tomatoes, peeled, seeded, and chopped
1 large bunch of fresh basil
7 oz/200 g zucchini, diced
7 oz/200 g green beans, chopped
2 oz/55 g dried vermicelli, broken into small pieces
salt and pepper

pesto sauce

3½ oz/100 g fresh basil leaves
2 large garlic cloves
1½ tbsp pine nuts
scant ¼ cup fruity extra virgin olive oil
2 oz/55 g/½ cup finely grated Parmesan cheese

method

1 If the fava beans are very young and tender, they can be used as they are. If they are older, use a small, sharp knife to slit the skins, then 'pop' out the green beans.

2 Heat the olive oil in a large heavy-bottom pan, over medium heat. Add the garlic, onion, celery, and carrot and sauté until the onion is soft, but not brown. Add the potatoes, stock, and tomatoes, and season with salt and pepper. Bring the stock to a boil, skimming the surface if necessary, then add the basil. Reduce the heat and cover the pan. Let simmer for 15 minutes, or until the potatoes are tender.

3 Meanwhile, make the pesto sauce. Whiz the basil, garlic, and pine nuts in a food processor or blender until a thick paste forms. Add the extra virgin olive oil and whiz again. Transfer to a bowl and stir in the cheese, then cover and chill until required.

4 When the potatoes are tender, stir the fava beans, zucchini, green beans, and vermicelli into the soup and continue simmering for 10 minutes, or until the vegetables are tender and the pasta is cooked. Adjust the seasoning if necessary. Remove the bunch of basil.

5 Ladle the soup into bowls and add a spoonful of pesto sauce to each bowl.

chicken & bean soup

ingredients

serves 4

2 tbsp butter
3 scallions, chopped
2 garlic cloves, finely chopped
1 fresh marjoram sprig, finely chopped
12 oz/350 g boneless chicken breasts, diced
2 pints/1.2 liters/5 cups chicken stock
12 oz/350 g canned chickpeas, drained and rinsed
1 bouquet garni
1 red bell pepper, diced
1 green bell pepper, diced
4 oz/115 g dried macaroni
salt and white pepper
croutons, to serve

method

1. Melt the butter in a large pan over medium heat. Add the scallions, garlic, marjoram, and chicken and cook, stirring frequently, for 5 minutes.

2. Add the stock, chickpeas, and bouquet garni, then season to taste with salt and white pepper. Bring the soup to a boil over medium heat, then reduce the heat and simmer for about 2 hours. Add the diced bell peppers and pasta to the pan, then simmer for an additional 20 minutes.

3. Ladle the soup into warmed serving bowls and sprinkle over the croutons. Serve immediately.

pasta niçoise

ingredients

serves 4

4 oz/115 g green beans, cut into 2-inch/5-cm lengths
8 oz/225 g dried fusilli tricolore
1/3 cup olive oil
2 tuna steaks, about 12 oz/350 g each
6 cherry tomatoes, halved
2 oz/55 g/1/3 cup black olives, pitted and halved
6 canned anchovies, drained and chopped
3 tbsp chopped fresh flat-leaf parsley
2 tbsp lemon juice
8–10 radicchio leaves
salt and pepper

method

1 Bring a large, heavy-bottom pan of lightly salted water to a boil. Add the green beans, reduce the heat, and cook for 5–6 minutes. Remove with a slotted spoon and refresh in a bowl of cold water. Drain well. Add the pasta to the same pan, return to a boil, and cook for 8–10 minutes, or until tender but still firm to the bite.

2 Meanwhile, brush a grill pan with some of the olive oil and heat until smoking. Season the tuna with salt and pepper and brush both sides with some of the remaining olive oil. Cook over medium heat for 2 minutes on each side, or until cooked to your liking, then remove from the grill pan and reserve.

3 Drain the pasta well and tip it into a bowl. Add the green beans, cherry tomatoes, olives, anchovies, parsley, lemon juice, and remaining olive oil and season with salt and pepper. Toss well and let cool. Remove and discard any skin from the tuna and slice thickly.

4 Gently mix the tuna into the pasta salad. Line a large salad bowl with the radicchio leaves, spoon in the salad, and serve.

tuna & herbed fusilli salad

ingredients

serves 4

7 oz/200 g dried fusilli
1 red bell pepper, seeded and cut into quarters
5½ oz/150 g asparagus spears
1 red onion, sliced
4 tomatoes, sliced
7 oz/200 g canned tuna in brine, drained and flaked

dressing

6 tbsp basil-flavored oil or extra virgin olive oil
3 tbsp white wine vinegar
1 tbsp lime juice
1 tsp mustard
1 tsp honey
4 tbsp chopped fresh basil, plus extra sprigs to garnish

method

1 Bring a large pan of lightly salted water to a boil. Add the pasta, return to a boil, and cook for 8–10 minutes until tender but still firm to the bite.

2 Meanwhile, put the bell pepper quarters under a preheated hot broiler and cook for 10–12 minutes until the skins begin to blacken. Transfer to a plastic bag, seal, and set aside.

3 Bring a separate pan of water to a boil, add the asparagus, and blanch for 4 minutes. Drain and plunge into cold water, then drain again. Remove the pasta from the heat, drain, and set aside to cool. Remove the bell pepper quarters from the bag and peel off the skins. Slice the bell pepper into strips.

4 To make the dressing, put all the dressing ingredients in a large bowl and stir together well. Add the pasta, bell pepper strips, asparagus, onion, tomatoes, and tuna. Toss together gently, then divide among serving bowls. Garnish with basil sprigs and serve.

orecchiette salad with pears & blue cheese

ingredients

serves 4

9 oz/250 g dried orecchiette
1 head of radicchio, torn into pieces
1 oak leaf lettuce, torn into pieces
2 pears
3 tbsp lemon juice
9 oz/250 g blue cheese, diced
2 oz/55 g/scant ½ cup chopped walnuts
4 tomatoes, cut into fourths
1 red onion, sliced
1 carrot, grated
8 fresh basil leaves
2 oz/55 g corn salad
4 tbsp olive oil
3 tbsp white wine vinegar
salt and pepper

method

1 Bring a large heavy-bottom pan of lightly salted water to a boil. Add the pasta, return to a boil, and cook for 8–10 minutes, or until tender but still firm to the bite. Drain, refresh in a bowl of cold water and drain again.

2 Place the radicchio and oak leaf lettuce leaves in a large bowl. Halve the pears, remove the cores, and dice the flesh. Toss the diced pear with 1 tablespoon of lemon juice in a small bowl to prevent discoloration. Top the salad with the blue cheese, walnuts, pears, pasta, tomatoes, onion slices, and grated carrot. Add the basil and corn salad.

3 Mix the remaining lemon juice and the olive oil and vinegar together in a measuring cup, then season with salt and pepper. Pour the dressing over the salad, toss, and serve immediately.

penne & apple salad

ingredients

serves 4

2 large heads of lettuce
9 oz/250 g dried penne
1 tbsp olive oil
8 red apples
juice of 4 lemons
1 stalk of celery, sliced
4 oz/115 g/¾ cup walnut halves
1 cup fresh garlic mayonnaise
salt

method

1 Wash and drain the lettuce leaves, then pat them dry with paper towels. Transfer them to the refrigerator for 1 hour, until crisp.

2 Meanwhile, bring a large pan of lightly salted water to a boil. Add the pasta and olive oil, bring back to a boil, and cook for 8–10 minutes, or until tender but still firm to the bite. Drain the pasta and refresh under cold running water. Drain thoroughly and set aside.

3 Core and dice the apples, then place them in a small bowl and sprinkle with the lemon juice to coat them thoroughly—this will prevent them from turning brown. Mix together the pasta, celery, apples, and walnut halves and toss the mixture in the garlic mayonnaise. Add more mayonnaise, to taste.

4 Line a salad bowl with the lettuce leaves and spoon the pasta salad into the lined bowl. Refrigerate until ready to serve.

warm pasta salad

ingredients

serves 4

- 8 oz/225 g dried farfalle or other pasta shapes
- 6 pieces of sun-dried tomato in oil, drained and chopped
- 4 scallions, chopped
- 2 oz/55 g arugula, shredded
- ½ cucumber, seeded and diced
- salt and pepper
- 2 tbsp freshly grated Parmesan cheese

dressing

- 4 tbsp olive oil
- ½ tsp superfine sugar
- 1 tbsp white wine vinegar
- 1 tsp Dijon mustard
- 4 fresh basil leaves, finely shredded
- salt and pepper

method

1. To make the dressing, whisk the olive oil, sugar, vinegar, and mustard together in a bowl. Season with salt and pepper, then stir in the basil.

2. Bring a large, heavy-bottom pan of lightly salted water to a boil. Add the pasta, return to a boil, and cook for 8–10 minutes, or until tender but still firm to the bite. Drain and transfer to a salad bowl. Add the dressing and toss well.

3. Add the chopped sun-dried tomatoes, scallions, arugula, and cucumber, season with salt and pepper, and toss. Sprinkle with the Parmesan cheese and serve warm.

pasta salad with bell peppers

ingredients

serves 4

1 red bell pepper
1 orange bell pepper
10 oz/280 g dried conchiglie
5 tbsp extra virgin olive oil
2 tbsp lemon juice
2 tbsp pesto
1 garlic clove, very finely chopped
3 tbsp shredded fresh basil leaves
salt and pepper

method

1 Put the whole bell peppers on a baking sheet and place under a preheated broiler, turning frequently, for 15 minutes, until charred all over. Remove with tongs and place in a bowl. Cover with crumpled paper towels and set aside.

2 Meanwhile, bring a large pan of lightly salted water to a boil. Add the pasta, bring back to a boil, and cook for 8–10 minutes, until tender but still firm to the bite.

3 Combine the olive oil, lemon juice, pesto, and garlic in a bowl, whisking well to mix. Drain the pasta, add it to the pesto mixture while still hot, and toss well. Set aside.

4 When the bell peppers are cool enough to handle, peel off the skins, then cut open and remove the seeds. Chop the flesh coarsely and add to the pasta with the basil. Season to taste with salt and pepper and toss well. Serve at room temperature.

spicy sausage pasta salad

ingredients

serves 4

4½ oz/125 g dried conchiglie
2 tbsp olive oil
1 medium onion, chopped
2 garlic cloves, very finely chopped
1 small yellow bell pepper, seeded and cut into very thin sticks
6 oz/175 g spicy pork sausage, such as chorizo, pepperoni, or salami, skinned and sliced
2 tbsp red wine
1 tbsp red wine vinegar
4 oz/125 g mixed salad greens
salt

method

1 Bring a large pan of lightly salted water to a boil over medium heat. Add the pasta and cook for 8–10 minutes, or until tender but still firm to the bite. Drain and set aside.

2 Heat the oil in a pan over medium heat. Add the onion and cook until translucent, then stir in the garlic, yellow bell pepper, and sausage, and cook for 3–4 minutes, stirring once or twice.

3 Add the wine, vinegar, and reserved pasta to the pan, stir, and bring the mixture just to a boil over medium heat.

4 Arrange the salad greens on serving plates, spoon over the warm sausage and pasta mixture, and serve immediately.

pasta salad with melon & shrimp

ingredients

serves 6

8 oz/225 g dried green fusilli
5 tbsp extra virgin olive oil
1 lb/450 g cooked shrimp
1 cantaloupe melon
1 honeydew melon
1 tbsp red wine vinegar
1 tsp whole grain mustard
pinch of superfine sugar
1 tbsp chopped fresh flat-leaf parsley
1 tbsp chopped fresh basil, plus extra sprigs to garnish
1 oak leaf lettuce, shredded
salt and pepper

method

1 Bring a large pan of salted water to a boil. Add the pasta, bring back to a boil, and cook for 8–10 minutes, or until tender but still firm to the bite. Drain, toss with 1 tablespoon of the olive oil, and let cool.

2 Meanwhile, peel and devein the shrimp, then place them in a large bowl. Halve both the melons and scoop out the seeds with a spoon. Using a melon baller or teaspoon, scoop out balls of the flesh and add them to the shrimp.

3 Whisk together the remaining olive oil, the vinegar, mustard, sugar, parsley, and basil in a small bowl. Season to taste with salt and pepper. Add the cooled pasta to the shrimp and melon mixture and toss lightly to mix, then pour in the dressing, and toss again. Cover with plastic wrap and chill in the refrigerator for 30 minutes.

4 Make a bed of shredded lettuce on a serving plate. Spoon the pasta salad on top, garnish with basil leaves, and serve.

meat & poultry

spaghetti bolognese

ingredients

serves 4

2 tbsp olive oil
1 tbsp butter
1 small onion, finely chopped
1 carrot, finely chopped
1 celery stalk, finely chopped
1¾ oz/50 g mushrooms, diced
8 oz/225 g ground beef
2¾ oz/75 g unsmoked bacon or ham, diced
2 chicken livers, chopped
2 tbsp tomato paste
4 fl oz/125 ml/½ cup dry white wine
½ tsp freshly grated nutmeg
10 fl oz/300 ml/1¼ cups chicken stock
4 fl oz/125 ml/½ cup heavy cream
1 lb/450 g dried spaghetti
salt and pepper
2 tbsp chopped fresh flat-leaf parsley, to garnish
freshly grated Parmesan cheese, to serve

method

1. Heat the olive oil and butter in a large pan over medium heat. Add the onion, carrot, celery, and mushrooms to the pan, then cook until soft. Add the beef and bacon and cook until the beef is evenly browned.

2. Stir in the chicken livers and tomato paste and cook for 2–3 minutes. Pour in the wine and season with salt, pepper, and the nutmeg. Add the stock. Bring to a boil, then cover and let simmer gently over low heat for 1 hour. Stir in the cream and simmer, uncovered, until reduced.

3. Bring a large pan of lightly salted water to a boil. Add the pasta, return to a boil, and cook until tender but still firm to the bite. Drain and transfer to a warmed serving dish.

4. Spoon the sauce over the pasta, garnish with parsley, and serve with Parmesan cheese.

spaghetti & meatballs

ingredients

serves 2

2 thick slices white bread, crusts removed
2 tbsp olive oil
1 red onion, chopped
2 garlic cloves, finely chopped
14 oz/400 g canned chopped tomatoes
8 basil leaves
2 tbsp tomato paste
1 tsp sugar
1 lb/450 g ground beef
2 eggs
1 tbsp chopped fresh parsley
1 tbsp chopped fresh basil
12 oz/350 g dried spaghetti
salt and pepper
freshly grated Parmesan cheese, to serve

method

1 Place the bread in a shallow bowl and add just enough water to cover. Soak for 5 minutes, then drain and squeeze the bread to remove all the liquid.

2 Heat the oil in a pan, add the onion and half the garlic, and cook over medium heat, stirring occasionally, for 5 minutes. Add the tomatoes with their juice, basil leaves, tomato paste, and sugar and season with salt and pepper. Bring to a boil, reduce the heat, and let simmer, stirring occasionally, for 20 minutes until thickened and pulpy.

3 Mix the bread, beef, eggs, remaining herbs, garlic, and ½ tsp of salt by hand in a large mixing bowl. Roll small pieces of the meat mixture into balls. Drop the meatballs into the tomato sauce, cover the pan, and cook over medium heat for 30 minutes.

4 Meanwhile, cook the spaghetti in a pan of lightly salted boiling water for 10 minutes, or until tender but still firm to the bite. Drain well.

5 Transfer the spaghetti to a large shallow serving bowl. Arrange the meatballs and sauce on top. Sprinkle 2 tablespoons of freshly grated Parmesan cheese over the top and serve with more cheese in a bowl on the side.

spaghetti alla carbonara

ingredients

serves 4

1 lb/450 g dried spaghetti
1 tbsp olive oil
8 oz/225 g rindless pancetta or lean bacon, chopped
4 eggs
5 tbsp light cream
4 tbsp freshly grated Parmesan cheese
salt and pepper

method

1. Bring a large, heavy-bottom pan of lightly salted water to a boil. Add the pasta, return to a boil, and cook for 8–10 minutes, or until tender but still firm to the bite.

2. Meanwhile, heat the olive oil in a heavy-bottom skillet. Add the chopped pancetta and cook over medium heat, stirring frequently, for 8–10 minutes.

3. Beat the eggs with the cream in a small bowl and season with salt and pepper. Drain the pasta and return it to the pan. Tip in the contents of the skillet, then add the egg mixture and half the Parmesan cheese. Stir well, then transfer to a warmed serving dish. Serve immediately, sprinkled with the remaining Parmesan cheese.

tagliatelle with a rich meat sauce

ingredients

serves 4

4 tbsp olive oil, plus extra for serving
3 oz/85 g pancetta or rindless lean bacon, diced
1 onion, chopped
1 garlic clove, finely chopped
1 carrot, chopped
1 celery stalk, chopped
8 oz/225 g/1 cup ground steak
4 oz/115 g chicken livers, chopped
2 tbsp strained tomatoes
4 fl oz/125 ml/½ cup dry white wine
8 fl oz/250 ml/1 cup beef stock or water
1 tbsp chopped fresh oregano
1 bay leaf
1 lb/450 g dried tagliatelle
salt and pepper
freshly grated Parmesan cheese, to serve

method

1 Heat the olive oil in a large, heavy-bottom pan. Add the pancetta or bacon and cook over medium heat, stirring occasionally, for 3–5 minutes, until it is just turning brown. Add the onion, garlic, carrot, and celery and cook, stirring occasionally, for an additional 5 minutes.

2 Add the steak and cook over high heat, breaking up the meat with a wooden spoon, for 5 minutes, until browned. Stir in the chicken livers and cook, stirring occasionally, for an additional 2–3 minutes. Add the strained tomatoes, wine, stock, oregano, and bay leaf, and season with salt and pepper. Bring to a boil, reduce the heat, cover, and let simmer for 30–35 minutes.

3 When the sauce is almost cooked, bring a large pan of lightly salted water to a boil. Add the pasta, bring back to a boil, and cook for 8–10 minutes, until tender but still firm to the bite. Drain, transfer to a warmed serving dish, drizzle with a little olive oil, and toss well.

4 Remove and discard the bay leaf from the sauce, then pour the sauce over the pasta, toss again, and serve immediately with grated Parmesan cheese.

chile pork with tagliatelle

ingredients

serves 4

1 lb/450 g dried tagliatelle
3 tbsp peanut oil
12 oz/350 g pork fillet, cut into thin strips
1 garlic clove, finely chopped
1 bunch of scallions, sliced
1-inch/2.5-cm piece fresh ginger, grated
2 fresh Thai chiles, seeded and finely chopped
1 red bell pepper, seeded and cut into thin sticks
1 yellow bell pepper, seeded and cut into thin sticks
3 zucchini, cut into thin sticks
2 tbsp finely chopped peanuts
1 tsp ground cinnamon
1 tbsp oyster sauce
2 oz/55 g creamed coconut, grated
salt and pepper
2 tbsp chopped fresh cilantro, to garnish

method

1 Bring a large heavy-bottom pan of lightly salted water to a boil. Add the pasta, return to a boil, and cook for 8–10 minutes, or until tender but still firm to the bite.

2 Meanwhile, heat the peanut oil in a preheated wok or large heavy-bottom skillet. Add the pork and stir-fry for 5 minutes. Add the garlic, scallions, ginger, and Thai chiles, and stir-fry for 2 minutes.

3 Add the red and yellow bell peppers and the zucchini and stir-fry for 1 minute. Add the peanuts, cinnamon, oyster sauce, and creamed coconut, and stir-fry for an additional 1 minute. Season with salt and pepper. Drain the pasta and transfer to a serving dish. Top with the chile pork, sprinkle with the chopped cilantro, and serve.

saffron linguine

ingredients

serves 4

12 oz/350 g dried linguine
pinch of saffron threads
2 tbsp water
5 oz/140 g ham, cut into strips
6 fl oz/175 ml/¾ cup heavy cream
2 oz/55 g/½ cup freshly grated Parmesan cheese
2 egg yolks
salt and pepper

method

1. Bring a large heavy-bottom pan of lightly salted water to a boil. Add the pasta, return to a boil, and cook for 8–10 minutes, or until tender but still firm to the bite.

2. Meanwhile, place the saffron in a separate heavy-bottom pan and add the water. Bring to a boil, then remove from the heat and let stand for 5 minutes.

3. Stir the ham, cream, and grated Parmesan cheese into the saffron and return the pan to the heat. Season with salt and pepper and heat through gently, stirring constantly, until simmering. Remove the pan from the heat and beat in the egg yolks. Drain the pasta and transfer to a large, warmed serving dish. Add the saffron sauce, toss well, and serve.

rigatoni with ham, tomato & chile sauce

ingredients

serves 4

1 tbsp olive oil
2 tbsp butter
1 onion, finely chopped
5½ oz/150 g ham, diced
2 garlic cloves, very finely chopped
1 fresh red chile, seeded and finely chopped
1 lb 12 oz/800 g canned chopped tomatoes
1 lb/450 g rigatoni or penne
2 tbsp chopped fresh flat-leaf parsley
6 tbsp freshly grated Parmesan cheese
salt and pepper

method

1. Put the olive oil and 1 tablespoon of the butter in a large pan over medium-low heat. Add the onion and fry for 10 minutes until soft and golden. Add the ham and fry for 5 minutes until lightly browned. Stir in the garlic, chile, and tomatoes. Season with a little salt and pepper. Bring to a boil, then let simmer over medium-low heat for 30–40 minutes until thickened.

2. Cook the pasta in plenty of boiling salted water until tender but still firm to the bite. Drain and transfer to a warmed serving dish.

3. Pour the sauce over the pasta. Add the parsley, Parmesan cheese, and the remaining butter. Toss well to mix and serve immediately.

farfalle with gorgonzola & ham

ingredients

serves 4

8 fl oz/225 ml/1 cup crème fraîche or sour cream
8 oz/225 g cremini mushrooms, quartered
14 oz/400 g dried farfalle
3 oz/85 g Gorgonzola cheese, crumbled
1 tbsp chopped fresh flat-leaf parsley, plus extra sprigs to garnish
1 cup cooked ham, diced
salt and pepper

method

1 Pour the crème fraîche into a pan, add the mushrooms, and season to taste with salt and pepper. Bring to just below a boil, then lower the heat, and simmer very gently, stirring occasionally, for 8–10 minutes, until the cream has thickened.

2 Meanwhile, bring a large pan of lightly salted water to a boil. Add the pasta, bring back to a boil, and cook for 8–10 minutes, until tender but still firm to the bite.

3 Remove the pan of mushrooms from the heat and stir in the Gorgonzola cheese until it has melted. Return the pan to very low heat and stir in the chopped parsley and ham.

4 Drain the pasta and add it to the sauce. Toss lightly, then divide among individual warmed dishes, garnish with the parsley sprigs, and serve.

variation

For a special occasion, omit the cooked ham and replace with 1 cup pancetta or bacon, diced.

pepperoni pasta

ingredients

serves 4

3 tbsp olive oil
1 onion, chopped
1 red bell pepper, seeded and diced
1 orange bell pepper, seeded and diced
1 lb 12 oz/800 g canned chopped tomatoes
1 tbsp sun-dried tomato paste
1 tsp paprika
8 oz/225 g pepperoni, sliced
2 tbsp chopped fresh flat-leaf parsley, plus extra to garnish
1 lb/450 g dried garganelli
salt and pepper
mixed salad greens, to serve

method

1 Heat 2 tablespoons of the olive oil in a large, heavy-bottom skillet. Add the onion and cook over low heat, stirring occasionally, for 5 minutes, or until softened. Add the red and orange bell peppers, tomatoes and their can juices, sun-dried tomato paste, and paprika to the pan and bring to a boil.

2 Add the pepperoni and parsley and season with salt and pepper. Stir well and bring to a boil, then reduce the heat and simmer for 10–15 minutes.

3 Meanwhile, bring a large, heavy-bottom pan of lightly salted water to a boil. Add the pasta, return to a boil, and cook for 8–10 minutes, or until tender but still firm to the bite.

4 Drain well and transfer to a warmed serving dish. Add the remaining olive oil and toss. Add the sauce and toss again. Sprinkle with parsley and serve immediately with mixed salad greens.

macaroni with sausage, pepperoncini & olives

ingredients

serves 4

1 tbsp olive oil
1 large onion, finely chopped
2 garlic cloves, minced
1 lb/450 g pork sausage, peeled and chopped coarsely
3 canned pepperoncini, or other hot red peppers, drained and sliced
14 oz/400 g canned chopped tomatoes
2 tsp dried oregano
4 fl oz/125 ml/½ cup chicken stock or red wine
1 lb/450 g dried macaroni
12–15 black olives, pitted and cut into fourths
2¾ oz/75 g/⅓ cup freshly grated cheese, such as Cheddar or Gruyère
salt and pepper

method

1. Heat the oil in a large skillet over medium heat. Add the onion and fry for 5 minutes until soft. Add the garlic and fry for a few seconds until just beginning to color. Add the sausage and fry until evenly browned.

2. Stir in the pepperoncini, tomatoes, oregano, and stock. Season with salt and pepper. Bring to a boil, then let simmer over medium heat for 10 minutes, stirring occasionally.

3. Cook the macaroni in plenty of boiling salted water until tender but still firm to the bite. Drain and transfer to a warmed serving dish.

4. Add the olives and half the cheese to the sauce, then stir until the cheese has melted. Pour the sauce over the pasta. Toss well to mix. Sprinkle with the remaining cheese and serve at once.

fusilli with bacon, eggs & mushrooms

ingredients

serves 4

1 tbsp olive oil
4 strips lean bacon or pancetta
4 oz/115 g/2 cups mushrooms, sliced
8 oz/225 g dried fusilli
2 eggs, beaten
4 oz/115 g Cheddar or mozzarella cheese, cubed
salt and pepper
chopped fresh flat-leaf parsley, to garnish

method

1 Heat the oil in a skillet over a medium heat. Add the bacon and cook until crisp. Remove with tongs, cut into small pieces and keep warm.

2 Cook the mushrooms in the pan with the bacon fat for 5–7 minutes, or until soft. Remove from the heat.

3 Cook the pasta in a pan of lightly salted boiling water for 8–10 minutes, or until tender but still firm to the bite.

4 Stir the mushrooms, beaten eggs, and the cheese cubes into the pasta. Season with pepper and toss until the eggs have coated the pasta and the cheese has melted.

5 Transfer to a warmed serving dish. Sprinkle with the bacon pieces and parsley and serve at once.

chorizo & mushroom pasta

ingredients

serves 6

1 lb 8 oz/680 g dried vermicelli
½ cup olive oil
2 garlic cloves, finely chopped
4½ oz/125 g chorizo, sliced
8 oz/225 g exotic mushrooms
3 fresh red chiles, chopped
2 tbsp fresh Parmesan cheese shavings, for sprinkling
10 anchovy fillets, to garnish
salt and pepper

method

1. Bring a large, heavy-bottom pan of lightly salted water to a boil. Add the vermicelli, return to a boil and cook for 8–10 minutes, or until just tender, but still firm to the bite. Drain the pasta thoroughly, then place on a large, warmed serving plate and keep warm.

2. Meanwhile, heat the olive oil in a skillet. Add the garlic and cook for 1 minute. Add the chorizo and exotic mushrooms and cook for 4 minutes. Add the chopped chiles and cook for an additional 1 minute.

3. Pour the chorizo and exotic mushroom mixture over the vermicelli and season with salt and pepper. Sprinkle with fresh Parmesan cheese shavings, garnish with anchovy fillets, and serve at once.

linguine with lamb & yellow bell pepper sauce

ingredients

serves 4

4 tbsp olive oil
10 oz/280 g boneless lamb, cubed
1 garlic clove, finely chopped
1 bay leaf
8 fl oz/125ml/1 cup dry white wine
2 large yellow bell peppers, seeded and diced
4 tomatoes, peeled and chopped
9 oz/250 g dried linguine
salt and pepper

method

1 Heat half the olive oil in a large heavy-bottom skillet. Add the lamb and cook over medium heat, stirring frequently, until browned on all sides. Add the garlic and cook for an additional 1 minute. Add the bay leaf, pour in the wine, and season with salt and pepper. Bring to a boil and cook for 5 minutes, or until reduced.

2 Stir in the remaining oil, bell peppers, and tomatoes. Reduce the heat, cover the pan, and let simmer, stirring occasionally, for 45 minutes.

3 Meanwhile, bring a large heavy-bottom pan of lightly salted water to a boil. Add the pasta, return to a boil, and cook for 8–10 minutes, or until tender but still firm to the bite. Drain and transfer to a warmed serving dish. Remove and discard the bay leaf from the lamb sauce and spoon the sauce onto the pasta. Toss well and serve immediately.

chicken with basil & pine nut pesto

ingredients

serves 4

2 tbsp vegetable oil
4 skinless, boneless chicken breasts
12 oz/350 g dried farfalle
salt and pepper
sprig of fresh basil, to garnish

pesto

3½ oz/100 g shredded fresh basil
½ cup extra virgin olive oil
3 tbsp pine nuts
3 garlic cloves, minced
2 oz/55 g freshly grated Parmesan cheese
2 tbsp freshly grated romano cheese

method

1 To make the pesto, place the basil, olive oil, pine nuts, garlic, and a generous pinch of salt in a food processor or blender and process until smooth. Scrape the mixture into a bowl and stir in the cheeses.

2 Heat the vegetable oil in a skillet over medium heat. Fry the chicken breasts, turning once, for 8–10 minutes until the juices are no longer pink. Cut into small cubes.

3 Cook the pasta in plenty of lightly salted boiling water until tender but still firm to the bite. Drain and transfer to a warmed serving dish. Add the chicken and pesto, then season with pepper. Toss well to mix. Garnish with a basil sprig and serve warm.

tagliatelle with creamy chicken & shiitake sauce

ingredients

serves 4

1 oz/25 g/⅓ cup dried shiitake mushrooms
12 fl oz/350 ml/1½ cups hot water
1 tbsp olive oil
6 bacon strips, chopped
3 boneless, skinless chicken breasts, sliced into strips
4 oz/115 g/2 cups fresh shiitake mushrooms, sliced
1 small onion, finely chopped
1 tsp fresh oregano or marjoram, finely chopped
9 fl oz/275 ml/generous 1 cup chicken stock
10 fl oz/300 ml/1¼ cups heavy cream
1 lb/450 g dried tagliatelle
2 oz/55 g/½ cup freshly grated Parmesan cheese
salt and pepper
chopped fresh flat-leaf parsley, to garnish

method

1 Put the dried mushrooms in a bowl with the hot water. Let soak for 30 minutes, or until softened. Remove, squeezing excess water back into the bowl. Strain the liquid in a fine-meshed strainer and reserve. Slice the soaked mushrooms, discarding the stems.

2 Heat the oil in a large skillet over a medium heat. Add the bacon and chicken, then stir-fry for about 3 minutes. Add the dried and fresh mushrooms, onion, and oregano. Stir-fry for 5–7 minutes, or until soft. Pour in the stock and the mushroom liquid. Bring to a boil, stirring. Simmer for about 10 minutes, continuing to stir, until reduced. Add the cream and simmer for 5 minutes, stirring, until beginning to thicken. Season with salt and pepper. Remove the skillet from the heat and set aside.

3 Cook the pasta until tender but still firm to the bite. Drain and transfer to a serving dish. Pour the sauce over the pasta. Add half the Parmesan cheese and mix. Sprinkle with parsley and serve with the remaining Parmesan cheese.

chicken with creamy penne

ingredients

serves 2

7 oz/200 g dried penne
1 tbsp olive oil
2 skinless, boneless chicken breasts
4 tbsp dry white wine
3/4 cup frozen peas
5 tbsp heavy cream
salt
4–5 tbsp chopped fresh parsley, to garnish

method

1 Bring a large saucepan of lightly salted water to a boil. Add the pasta, bring back to a boil, and cook for about 8–10 minutes, or according to the package directions, until tender but still firm to the bite.

2 Meanwhile, heat the oil in a skillet, add the chicken, and cook over medium heat for about 4 minutes on each side.

3 Pour in the wine and cook over high heat until it has almost evaporated. Drain the pasta. Add the peas, cream, and pasta to the skillet and stir well. Cover and simmer for 2 minutes. Garnish with fresh parsley and serve.

italian chicken spirals

ingredients

serves 4

4 skinless, boneless chicken breasts
1 oz/25 g/1 cup fresh basil leaves
15 g/½ oz/1 tbsp hazelnuts
1 garlic clove, crushed
9 oz/250 g dried
whole wheat fusilli
2 sun-dried tomatoes or fresh
tomatoes
1 tbsp lemon juice
1 tbsp olive oil
1 tbsp capers
2 oz/55 g/½ cup pitted black olives
salt and pepper

method

1 Beat the chicken breasts with a rolling pin to flatten evenly. Place the basil and hazelnuts in a food processor and process until finely chopped. Mix with the garlic and salt and pepper to taste.

2 Spread the basil mixture over the chicken breasts and roll up from one short end to enclose the filling. Wrap the chicken rolls tightly in foil so that they hold their shape, then seal the ends well.

3 Bring a pan of lightly salted water to a boil and cook the pasta for 8–10 minutes, or until tender but still firm to the bite. Meanwhile, place the chicken parcels in a steamer or colander set over the pan, cover tightly, and steam for 10 minutes.

4 Using a sharp knife, dice the tomatoes. Drain the pasta and return to the pan with the lemon juice, oil, tomatoes, capers, and olives. Warm through.

5 Pierce the chicken with a skewer to make sure that the juices run clear. Slice the chicken, arrange over the pasta in a warm serving dish and serve.

seafood

conchiglie with smoked salmon & sour cream

ingredients

serves 4

- 1 lb/450 g dried conchiglie
- 10 fl oz/300 ml/1¼ cups sour cream
- 2 tsp whole grain mustard
- 4 large scallions, finely sliced
- 8 oz/225 g smoked salmon, cut into bite-size pieces
- finely grated rind of ½ lemon
- salt and pepper
- 2 tbsp snipped fresh chives, to garnish

method

1. Bring a large, heavy-based saucepan of lightly salted water to a boil. Add the pasta, return to a boil and cook for 8–10 minutes, or until tender but still firm to the bite. Drain and return to the pan.

2. Add the sour cream, mustard, scallions, smoked salmon, and lemon rind to the pasta. Stir over a low heat until heated through. Season to taste with pepper.

3. Transfer to a warmed serving dish and garnish with the chives. Serve warm or at room temperature.

fettuccine with sole & monkfish

ingredients

serves 4

3 oz/85 g/generous ½ cup all-purpose flour
1 lb/450 g lemon sole fillets, skinned and cut into chunks
1 lb/450 g monkfish fillets, skinned and cut into chunks
5 tbsp unsalted butter
4 shallots, finely chopped
2 garlic cloves, crushed
1 carrot, diced
1 leek, finely chopped
10 fl oz/300 ml/1¼ cups fish stock
10 fl oz/300 ml/1¼ cups dry white wine
2 tsp anchovy essence
1 tbsp balsamic vinegar
1 lb/450 g dried fettuccine
salt and pepper
chopped fresh flat-leaf parsley, to garnish

method

1 Season the flour with salt and pepper and spread out 2 tablespoons on a plate. Coat all the fish pieces with it, shaking off the excess. Melt the butter in a heavy-bottom pan or flameproof casserole. Add the fish, shallots, garlic, carrot, and leek, then cook over low heat, stirring frequently, for 10 minutes. Sprinkle in the remaining seasoned flour and cook, stirring constantly, for 1 minute.

2 Mix the fish stock, wine, anchovy essence, and balsamic vinegar together in a pitcher and gradually stir into the fish mixture. Bring to a boil, stirring constantly, then reduce the heat and let simmer gently for 35 minutes.

3 Meanwhile, bring a large heavy-bottom pan of lightly salted water to a boil. Add the pasta, return to a boil, and cook for 8–10 minutes, or until tender but still firm to the bite. Drain and transfer to a warmed serving dish. Spoon the fish mixture onto the pasta, garnish with chopped parsley, and serve immediately.

mafalde with fresh salmon

ingredients

serves 4

12 oz/350 g salmon fillet
fresh dill sprigs, plus extra to garnish
8 fl oz/125ml/1 cup dry white wine
6 tomatoes, peeled and chopped
5 fl oz/150 ml/2/3 cup heavy cream
12 oz/350 g dried mafalde, tagliatelle, or fettuccine
4 oz/115 g cooked, shelled shrimp
salt and pepper

method

1 Place the salmon in a large heavy-bottom skillet. Add a few dill sprigs, pour in the wine, and season with salt and pepper. Bring to a boil, then reduce the heat, cover, and poach gently for 5 minutes, or until the flesh flakes easily. Remove with a spatula, reserving the cooking liquid, and let cool slightly. Remove and discard the skin and any remaining small bones, then flake the flesh into large chunks.

2 Add the tomatoes and cream to the reserved liquid. Bring to a boil, then reduce the heat and let simmer for 15 minutes, or until the sauce has thickened.

3 Meanwhile, bring a large heavy-bottom pan of lightly salted water to a boil. Add the pasta, return to a boil, and cook for 8–10 minutes, or until tender but still firm to the bite. Drain and transfer to a warmed serving dish.

4 Add the salmon and shrimp to the tomato sauce and stir gently until coated. Spoon the sauce onto the pasta, toss lightly, then serve, garnished with dill sprigs.

linguine with smoked salmon & arugula

ingredients

serves 4

12 oz/350 g dried linguine
2 tbsp olive oil
1 garlic clove, finely chopped
4 oz/115 g smoked salmon, cut into thin strips
2 oz/55 g arugula
salt and pepper
4 lemon halves, to garnish

method

1. Bring a large, heavy-bottom pan of lightly salted water to a boil. Add the pasta, return to a boil, and cook for 8–10 minutes, or until tender but still firm to the bite.

2. Just before the end of the cooking time, heat the olive oil in a heavy-bottom skillet. Add the garlic and cook over low heat, stirring constantly, for 1 minute. Do not allow the garlic to brown or it will taste bitter. Add the salmon and arugula. Season with salt and pepper and cook, stirring constantly, for 1 minute. Remove the skillet from the heat.

3. Drain the pasta and transfer to a warmed dish. Add the smoked salmon and arugula mixture, toss lightly and serve, garnished with lemon halves.

fusilli with monkfish & broccoli

ingredients

serves 4

4 oz/115 g head of broccoli, divided into florets
3 tbsp olive oil
12 oz/350 g monkfish fillet, skinned and cut into bite-size pieces
2 garlic cloves, crushed
4 fl oz/125 ml/½ cup dry white wine
8 fl oz/225 ml/1 cup heavy cream
14 oz/400 g dried fusilli bucati
3 oz/85 g Gorgonzola cheese, diced
salt and pepper

method

1 Divide the broccoli florets into tiny sprigs. Bring a pan of lightly salted water to a boil, add the broccoli, and cook for 2 minutes. Drain and refresh under cold running water.

2 Heat the olive oil in a large heavy-bottom skillet. Add the monkfish and garlic and season with salt and pepper. Cook, stirring frequently, for 5 minutes, or until the fish is opaque. Pour in the white wine and cream and cook, stirring occasionally, for 5 minutes, or until the fish is cooked through and the sauce has thickened. Stir in the broccoli sprigs.

3 Meanwhile, bring a large heavy-bottom pan of lightly salted water to a boil. Add the pasta, return to a boil, and cook the pasta for 8–10 minutes, or until tender but still firm to the bite. Drain the pasta and tip it into the pan with the fish, add the cheese, and toss lightly. Serve immediately.

linguine alla puttanesca

ingredients

serves 4

1 lb/450 g plum tomatoes
3 tbsp olive oil
2 garlic cloves, finely chopped
10 anchovy fillets, drained and chopped
5 oz/140 g/¾ cup black olives, pitted and chopped
1 tbsp capers, rinsed
pinch of cayenne pepper
14 oz/400 g dried linguine
salt
2 tbsp chopped fresh flat-leaf parsley, to garnish
crusty bread, to serve

method

1 Peel the tomatoes by cutting a cross in the bottom of each and placing in a heatproof bowl. Cover with boiling water and let stand for 35–45 seconds. Drain and plunge into cold water, then the skins will slide off easily. Seed and chop the tomatoes.

2 Heat the olive oil in a heavy-bottom pan. Add the garlic and cook over low heat, stirring frequently, for 2 minutes. Add the anchovies and mash them to a pulp with a fork. Add the olives, capers, and tomatoes and season with cayenne pepper. Cover and let simmer for 25 minutes.

3 Meanwhile, bring a pan of lightly salted water to a boil. Add the pasta, return to a boil, and cook for 8–10 minutes, or until tender but still firm to the bite. Drain and transfer to a warmed serving dish.

4 Spoon the anchovy sauce into the dish and toss the pasta, using 2 large forks. Garnish with the parsley and serve immediately with crusty bread.

pasta with tuna, garlic, lemon, capers & olives

ingredients

serves 4

12 oz/350 g dried conchiglie or gnocchi
4 tbsp olive oil
4 tbsp butter
3 large garlic cloves, thinly sliced
7 oz/200 g canned tuna, drained and broken into chunks
2 tbsp lemon juice
1 tbsp capers, drained
10–12 black olives, pitted and sliced
2 tbsp chopped fresh flat-leaf parsley
mixed leaves, to serve

method

1 Cook the pasta or gnocchi in plenty of boiling salted water until tender but still firm to the bite. Drain and return to the pan.

2 Heat the olive oil and half the butter in a skillet over medium-low heat. Add the garlic and cook for a few seconds until just beginning to color. Reduce the heat to low. Add the tuna, lemon juice, capers, and olives. Stir gently until all the ingredients are heated through.

3 Transfer the pasta or gnocchi to a warmed serving dish. Pour the tuna mixture over the pasta. Add the parsley and remaining butter. Toss well to mix, then serve immediately with mixed leaves.

spinach & anchovy pasta

ingredients

serves 4

2 lb/900 g fresh, young spinach leaves
14 oz/400 g dried fettuccine
5 tbsp olive oil
3 tbsp pine nuts
3 garlic cloves, crushed
8 canned anchovy fillets, drained and chopped

method

1 Trim off any tough spinach stalks. Rinse the spinach leaves under cold running water and place them in a large pan with only the water that is clinging to them after washing. Cover and cook over high heat, shaking the pan from time to time, until the spinach has wilted, but retains its color. Drain well, set aside, and keep warm.

2 Bring a large heavy-bottom pan of lightly salted water to a boil. Add the fettuccine, return to a boil and cook for 8–10 minutes, or until it is just tender but still firm to the bite.

3 Heat 4 tablespoons of the olive oil in a separate pan. Add the pine nuts and cook until golden. Remove the pine nuts from the pan and set aside.

4 Add the garlic to the pan and cook until golden. Add the anchovies and stir in the spinach. Cook, stirring, for 2–3 minutes, until heated through. Return the pine nuts to the pan.

5 Drain the fettuccine, toss in the remaining olive oil and transfer to a warmed serving dish. Spoon the anchovy and spinach sauce over the fettuccine, toss lightly, and serve at once.

penne with squid & tomatoes

ingredients

serves 4

8 oz/225 g dried penne
12 oz/350 g prepared squid
6 tbsp olive oil
2 onions, sliced
1 cup fish stock or chicken stock
5 fl oz/150 ml/2/3 cup full-bodied red wine
14 oz/400 g canned chopped tomatoes
2 tbsp tomato paste
1 tbsp chopped fresh marjoram
1 bay leaf
salt and pepper
2 tbsp chopped fresh flat-leaf parsley, to garnish

method

1 Bring a large, heavy-bottom pan of lightly salted water to a boil. Add the pasta, return to a boil, and cook for 3 minutes, then drain and set aside until ready to use. With a sharp knife, cut the squid into strips.

2 Heat the olive oil in a large saucepan. Add the onions and cook over low heat, stirring occasionally, for 5 minutes, or until softened. Add the squid and stock, bring to a boil, and simmer for 3 minutes. Stir in the wine, chopped tomatoes and their can juices, tomato paste, marjoram, and bay leaf. Season to taste with salt and pepper. Bring to a boil and cook for 5 minutes, or until slightly reduced.

3 Add the pasta, return to a boil, and simmer for 8–10 minutes, or until tender but still firm to the bite. Remove and discard the bay leaf. Transfer to a warmed serving dish, sprinkle with the parsley, and serve immediately.

linguine with shrimp & scallops

ingredients

serves 6

1 lb/450 g raw shrimp
2 tbsp butter
2 shallots, finely chopped
1 cup dry white vermouth
12 fl oz/350 ml/1½ cups water
1 lb/450 g dried linguine
2 tbsp olive oil
1 lb/450 g prepared scallops
2 tbsp chopped fresh chives
salt and pepper

method

1 Shell and devein the shrimp, reserving the shells. Melt the butter in a heavy-bottom skillet. Add the shallots and cook over low heat, stirring occasionally, for 5 minutes, or until softened. Add the shrimp shells and cook, stirring constantly, for 1 minute. Pour in the vermouth and cook, stirring, for 1 minute. Add the water, bring to a boil, then reduce the heat and let simmer for 10 minutes, or until the liquid has reduced by half. Remove the skillet from the heat.

2 Bring a large heavy-bottom pan of lightly salted water to a boil. Add the pasta, return to a boil, and cook for 8–10 minutes, or until tender but still firm to the bite.

3 Meanwhile, heat the oil in a separate heavy-bottom skillet. Add the scallops and shrimp and cook, stirring frequently, for 2 minutes, or until the scallops are opaque and the shrimp have changed color. Strain the shrimp-shell stock into the skillet. Drain the pasta and add to the skillet with the chives and season to taste with salt and pepper. Toss well over low heat for 1 minute, then serve.

tagliatelle & mussels with white wine, garlic & parsley

ingredients

serves 4

4 lb 8 oz/2 kilos mussels, scrubbed*
1 large onion, chopped
3 garlic cloves, minced
18 fl oz/550 ml/2¼ cups dry white wine
1 bay leaf
2 sprigs of fresh thyme
5 tbsp chopped fresh flat-leaf parsley
1 tbsp chopped fresh rosemary
4 tbsp butter
1 lb/450 g dried tagliatelle or other broad-ribboned pasta
salt and pepper

* discard any damaged mussels or any that do not shut immediately when tapped; once cooked, discard any mussels that remain closed

method

1. Clean the mussels by scrubbing the shells and pulling out any beards that are attached. Rinse well, discarding any mussels with broken shells or that remain open when tapped.
2. Put the onion, garlic, white wine, herbs, and 2 tablespoons of the butter in a pan. Bring to a boil, then reduce the heat. Add the mussels, then season with salt and pepper. Cover and cook over medium heat for 3–4 minutes, shaking the pan, until the mussels open. Remove from the heat. Lift out the mussels with a perforated spoon, reserving the liquid. Discard any that remain closed. Remove most of the others from their shells, reserving a few in their shells to garnish.
3. Cook the pasta until tender but still firm to the bite, then drain it and divide it among 4 individual serving bowls. Spoon the mussels over the pasta. Strain the mussel liquid and return to the pan. Add the remaining butter and heat until melted. Pour over the pasta, garnish with the mussels in their shells, and serve immediately.

mixed shellfish with angel-hair pasta

ingredients

serves 4

3 oz/85 g prepared squid
1 tsp cornstarch
1 tbsp water
1 egg white
4 prepared scallops, sliced
3 oz/85 g raw shrimp, shelled and deveined
12 oz/350 g angel-hair pasta
3 tbsp peanut oil
2 oz/55 g snow peas
1 tbsp dark soy sauce
1 tbsp dry sherry
½ tsp light brown sugar
2 scallions, shredded
salt

method

1 Open out the squid and, with a sharp knife, score the inside with criss-cross lines. Cut into small pieces, about ¾-inch/2-cm square. Place in a bowl and cover with boiling water. When the squares have curled up, drain and rinse in cold water. Mix the cornstarch and water together in a small bowl until a smooth paste forms and stir in about half the egg white. Add the scallops and shrimp and toss until well coated.

2 Bring a large heavy-bottom pan of lightly salted water to a boil. Add the pasta, return to a boil, and cook for 5 minutes, or until tender but still firm to the bite.

3 Meanwhile, heat the oil in a preheated wok or heavy-bottom skillet. Add the snow peas, squid, scallops, and shrimp, and stir-fry for 2 minutes. Stir in the soy sauce, sherry, sugar, and scallions, and cook, stirring, for 1 minute. Drain the pasta and divide it among 4 warmed plates. Top with the shellfish mixture and serve at once.

fettuccine with scallops in porcini & cream sauce

ingredients

serves 4

1 oz/25 g dried porcini mushrooms
18 fl oz/550 ml/2¼ cups hot water
3 tbsp olive oil
3 tbsp butter
12 oz/350 g scallops, sliced
2 garlic cloves, very finely chopped
2 tbsp lemon juice
9 fl oz/250 ml/generous 1 cup heavy cream
12 oz/350 g dried fettuccine or pappardelle
salt and pepper
2 tbsp chopped fresh flat-leaf parsley, to serve

method

1. Put the porcini and hot water in a bowl and let soak for 20 minutes. Strain the mushrooms, reserving the soaking water, and chop coarsely. Line a strainer with paper towels and strain the mushroom water into a bowl.

2. Heat the oil and butter in a large skillet over medium heat. Add the scallops and cook for 2 minutes until just golden. Add the garlic and mushrooms and stir-fry for 1 minute.

3. Stir in the lemon juice, cream, and 4 fl oz/125 ml/ ½ cup of the mushroom water. Bring to a boil, then let simmer over medium heat for 2–3 minutes, stirring constantly, until the liquid is reduced by half. Season with salt and pepper. Remove from the heat.

4. Cook the pasta in plenty of boiling salted water until tender but still firm to the bite. Drain and transfer to a warmed serving dish. Briefly reheat the sauce and pour over the pasta. Sprinkle with the parsley and toss well to mix. Serve at once.

seafood pasta pockets

ingredients

serves 4

2 tbsp extra virgin olive oil
2 fresh red chiles, seeded and finely chopped
4 garlic cloves, finely chopped
1 lb 12 oz/800 g canned tomatoes
8 fl oz/225ml/1 cup dry white wine
12 oz/350 g dried spaghetti
2 tbsp butter
4 oz/115 g prepared raw squid, sliced
6 oz/175 g raw jumbo shrimp
1 lb/450 g live mussels, scrubbed and debearded*
1 crab, about 3 lb 5 oz/1.5 kg, freshly cooked, all meat removed
3 tbsp coarsely chopped fresh flat-leaf parsley
1 tbsp shredded fresh basil leaves
salt and pepper

* discard any damaged mussels or any that do not shut immediately when tapped; once cooked, discard any mussels that remain closed

method

1 Heat 1 tablespoon of the olive oil in a large pan. Add half the chiles and half the garlic, and cook over medium heat, stirring occasionally, for 2–3 minutes. Add the tomatoes with their can juices and the wine. Reduce the heat and let simmer for about 1 hour. Strain the sauce, season, and set aside.

2 Bring a pan of lightly salted water to a boil. Add the pasta, return to a boil, and cook for 8–10 minutes, until tender but still firm to the bite.

3 Heat the remaining olive oil with the butter in a large, heavy-bottom pan. Add the remaining chile and garlic and cook over low heat, stirring occasionally, for 5 minutes, or until softened. Add the squid, shrimp, and mussels, cover the pan, and cook over high heat for 4–5 minutes, or until the mussels have opened. Remove the pan from the heat and stir in the crab meat. Drain the pasta and add it to the seafood with the chile and tomato sauce, parsley, and basil.

4 Cut out 4 large squares of parchment paper. Divide the pasta and seafood among them, placing it on one half. Fold over the other half and turn in the edges securely to seal. Transfer to a large cookie sheet and bake in a preheated oven, 350°F/180°C, for 10 minutes, or until the pockets have puffed up. Serve at once.

springtime pasta

ingredients

serves 4

2 tbsp lemon juice
4 baby globe artichokes
7 tbsp olive oil
2 shallots, finely chopped
2 garlic cloves, finely chopped
2 tbsp chopped fresh flat-leaf parsley
2 tbsp chopped fresh mint
12 oz/350 g dried rigatoni or other tubular pasta
2 tbsp unsalted butter
12 large raw shrimp, shelled and deveined
salt and pepper

method

1 Fill a large bowl with cold water and add the lemon juice. Prepare the artichokes one at a time. Cut off the stems and trim away any tough outer leaves. Cut across the tops of the leaves. Slice in half lengthwise and remove the central fibrous chokes, then cut lengthwise into slices ¼ inch/5 mm thick. Immediately place the artichoke slices in the bowl of acidulated water to prevent discoloration.

2 Heat 5 tablespoons of the olive oil in a heavy-bottom skillet. Drain the artichoke slices and pat dry with paper towels. Add them to the skillet with the shallots, garlic, parsley, and mint and cook over low heat, stirring frequently, for 10–12 minutes, or until tender.

3 Meanwhile, bring a large pan of lightly salted water to a boil. Add the pasta, return to a boil, and cook for 8–10 minutes, or until tender but still firm to the bite.

4 Melt the butter in a skillet, cut the shrimp in half, and add them to the skillet. Cook, stirring occasionally, for 2–3 minutes, or until the shrimp have changed color. Season with salt and pepper.

5 Drain the pasta and tip it into a bowl. Add the remaining olive oil and toss well. Add the artichoke mixture and the shrimp and toss again. Serve immediately.

spaghetti with shrimp & garlic sauce

ingredients

serves 4

3 tbsp olive oil
3 tbsp butter
4 garlic cloves, minced
2 tbsp finely diced red bell pepper
2 tbsp tomato paste
4 fl oz/125 ml/½ cup dry white wine
1 lb/450 g spaghetti or tagliatelle
12 oz/350 g raw shelled shrimp
4 fl oz/125 ml/½ cup heavy cream
salt and pepper
3 tbsp chopped fresh flat-leaf parsley, to garnish

method

1 Heat the oil and butter in a pan over medium-low heat. Add the garlic and red bell pepper. Fry for a few seconds until the garlic is just beginning to color. Stir in the tomato paste and wine. Cook for 10 minutes, stirring.

2 Cook the spaghetti in plenty of boiling salted water until tender but still firm to the bite. Drain and return to the pan.

3 Add the shrimp to the sauce and raise the heat to medium-high. Cook for 2 minutes, stirring, until the shrimp turn pink. Reduce the heat and stir in the cream. Cook for 1 minute, stirring constantly, until thickened. Season with salt and pepper.

4 Transfer the spaghetti to a warmed serving dish and pour over the sauce. Sprinkle with the parsley. Toss well to mix and serve at once.

spaghetti with clams

ingredients

serves 4

2 lb 4 oz/1 kg live clams, scrubbed under cold running water*
6 fl oz/175 ml/¾ cup water
6 fl oz/175 ml/¾ cup dry white wine
12 oz/350 g dried spaghetti
5 tbsp olive oil
2 garlic cloves, finely chopped
4 tbsp chopped fresh flat-leaf parsley
salt and pepper

* discard any damaged clams or any that do not shut immediately when tapped; once cooked, discard any clams that remain closed

method

1 Place the clams in a large, heavy-bottom pan, add the water and wine, cover, and cook over high heat, shaking the pan occasionally, for 5 minutes, or until the shells have opened.

2 Remove the clams with a slotted spoon and let cool slightly. Strain the cooking liquid, through a strainer lined with cheesecloth, into a small pan. Bring to a boil and cook until reduced by about half, then remove from the heat. Meanwhile, discard any clams that have not opened, remove the remainder from their shells, and reserve until required.

3 Bring a large pan of lightly salted water to a boil. Add the pasta, return to a boil, and cook for 8–10 minutes, or until tender but still firm to the bite.

4 Meanwhile, heat the olive oil in a large, heavy-bottom skillet. Add the garlic and cook, stirring frequently, for 2 minutes. Add the parsley and the reduced clam cooking liquid and let simmer gently.

5 Drain the pasta and add it to the skillet with the clams. Season with salt and pepper and cook, stirring constantly, for 4 minutes, or until the pasta is coated and the clams have heated through. Transfer to a warmed serving dish and serve immediately.

spaghetti & shellfish

ingredients

serves 4

8 oz/225 g dried short-cut spaghetti, or long spaghetti broken into 6-inch/15-cm lengths
1 tbsp olive oil
10 fl oz/300 ml/1¼ cups chicken stock
1 tsp lemon juice
1 small cauliflower, cut into florets
2 carrots, sliced thinly
4½ oz/125 g snow peas
4 tbsp butter
1 onion, sliced
8 oz/225 g zucchini, sliced thinly
1 garlic clove, chopped
12 oz/350 g frozen shelled shrimp, thawed
2 tbsp chopped fresh parsley
1 oz/25 g/¼ cup freshly grated Parmesan cheese
salt and pepper
½ tsp paprika, to sprinkle
4 unshelled shrimp, to garnish (optional)
crusty bread, to serve

method

1 Bring a large, heavy-bottom pan of lightly salted water to a boil. Add the spaghetti, return to a boil and cook for 8–10 minutes, or until tender but still firm to the bite. Drain, then return to the pan and stir in the olive oil. Cover and keep warm.

2 Bring the chicken stock and lemon juice to a boil. Add the cauliflower and carrots and cook for 3–4 minutes, until they are tender. Remove with a slotted spoon and set aside. Add the snow peas and cook for 1–2 minutes, until they start to soften. Remove and add to the other vegetables. Reserve the stock for future use.

3 Melt half of the butter in a skillet over medium heat and cook the onion and zucchini for 3 minutes. Add the garlic and shrimp and cook for an additional 2–3 minutes, until thoroughly heated through.

4 Stir in the reserved vegetables and heat through. Season with salt and pepper, then stir in the remaining butter. Transfer the spaghetti to a warmed serving dish. Pour on the sauce and parsley. Toss well using 2 forks, until thoroughly coated. Sprinkle on the grated cheese and paprika, and garnish with unshelled shrimp, if using. Serve immediately, with crusty bread.

vegetarian

tagliatelle with pesto

ingredients

serves 4

1 lb/450 g dried tagliatelle
salt
fresh basil sprigs, to garnish

pesto

2 garlic cloves
1 oz/25 g/¼ cup pine nuts
4 oz/115 g fresh basil leaves
½ cup olive oil
2 oz/55 g/½ cup freshly grated Parmesan cheese
salt

method

1 To make the pesto, put the garlic, pine nuts, and a large pinch of salt into a food processor or blender and process briefly. Add the basil leaves and process to a paste. With the motor still running, gradually add the oil. Scrape into a bowl and beat in the Parmesan cheese. Season to taste with salt.

2 Bring a large pan of lightly salted water to a boil. Add the pasta, return to a boil, and cook for 8–10 minutes, or until tender but still firm to the bite. Drain the pasta well, return to the pan, and toss with half the pesto, then divide among warmed serving dishes and top with the remaining pesto. Garnish with basil and serve immediately.

variation

Use red pesto instead of green pesto for something a bit different. To make the pesto put 4½ oz/125 g sun-dried tomatoes, 2 crushed garlic cloves, 4 tablespoons of lightly toasted pine nuts and 5 fl oz/150 ml extra virgin olive oil into a food processor and blend to a coarse paste. Use as above.

paglia e fieno with garlic crumbs

ingredients

serves 4

- 12 oz/350 g/6 cups fresh white bread crumbs
- 4 tbsp finely chopped fresh flat-leaf parsley
- 1 tbsp chopped fresh chives
- 2 tbsp finely chopped fresh sweet marjoram
- 3 tbsp olive oil, plus extra to serve
- 3–4 garlic cloves, finely chopped
- 2 oz/55 g/½ cup pine nuts
- 1 lb/450 g fresh paglia e fieno
- salt and pepper
- 2 oz/55 g/½ cup freshly grated romano cheese, to serve

method

1. Mix the bread crumbs, parsley, chives, and marjoram together in a small bowl. Heat the olive oil in a large heavy-bottom skillet. Add the bread crumb mixture and the garlic and pine nuts, season with salt and pepper, and cook over low heat, stirring constantly, for 5 minutes, or until the bread crumbs become golden, but not crisp. Remove the skillet from the heat and cover to keep warm.

2. Bring a large heavy-bottom pan of lightly salted water to a boil. Add the pasta, return to a boil, and cook for 4–5 minutes, or until tender but still firm to the bite.

3. Drain the pasta and transfer to a warmed serving dish. Drizzle with 2–3 tablespoons of olive oil and toss to mix. Add the garlic bread crumbs and toss again. Serve immediately with the grated romano cheese.

fettuccine alfredo

ingredients

serves 4

2 tbsp butter
7 fl oz/225 ml/scant 1 cup
heavy cream
1 lb/450 g fresh fettuccine
1 tbsp olive oil
3¼ oz/90 g/generous ¾ cup freshly
grated Parmesan cheese,
plus extra to serve
pinch of freshly grated nutmeg
salt and pepper
fresh flat-leaf parsley sprigs,
to garnish

method

1 Place the butter and 5 fl oz/150 ml/⅔ cup of the cream in a large pan and bring the mixture to a boil over medium heat. Reduce the heat and let simmer gently for about 1½ minutes, or until slightly thickened.

2 Meanwhile, bring a large pan of lightly salted water to a boil. Add the fettuccine and oil, return to a boil and cook for 2–3 minutes until tender but still firm to the bite. Drain the fettuccine, return it to the pan and pour the sauce over it. Return the pan to low heat and toss the fettuccine in the sauce until coated.

3 Add the remaining cream, the Parmesan cheese, and nutmeg to the fettuccine mixture and season with salt and pepper. Toss thoroughly to coat while gently heating through.

4 Transfer the fettuccine mixture to a warmed serving plate and garnish with parsley sprigs. Serve the dish immediately, with extra grated Parmesan cheese.

fettuccine with ricotta

ingredients

serves 4

12 oz/350 g dried fettuccine
3 tbsp unsalted butter
2 tbsp chopped fresh flat-leaf parsley, plus extra leaves to garnish
4 oz/115 g/generous ½ cup ricotta cheese
4 oz/115 g/generous 1 cup ground almonds
5 fl oz/150 ml/⅔ cup sour cream
2 tbsp extra virgin olive oil
4 fl oz/125 ml/½ cup vegetable stock
pinch of freshly grated nutmeg
salt and pepper
1 tbsp pine nuts

method

1 Bring a large heavy-bottom pan of lightly salted water to a boil. Add the pasta, return to a boil, and cook for 8–10 minutes, or until tender but still firm to the bite. Drain well and return to the pan. Add the butter and chopped parsley and toss thoroughly to coat.

2 Mix the ricotta, ground almonds, and sour cream together in a bowl. Gradually stir in the olive oil, followed by the hot vegetable stock. Season with nutmeg and pepper.

3 Transfer the pasta to a warmed dish, pour over the sauce, and toss. Sprinkle with pine nuts, garnish with parsley leaves, and serve immediately.

fettuccine with garlic, tomatoes & olives

ingredients

serves 4

4 plum tomatoes, peeled, seeded, and chopped
4 garlic cloves, finely chopped
8 black olives, pitted and finely chopped
1 red chile, seeded and finely chopped
2 tbsp chopped fresh flat-leaf parsley
2 tbsp extra virgin olive oil
1 tbsp lemon juice
10 oz/280 g dried fettuccine
salt and pepper

method

1 Place the tomatoes in a large, nonmetallic strainer set over a bowl. Cover and set aside in the refrigerator for 30 minutes.

2 Combine the garlic, olives, chile, parsley, oil, and lemon juice in a separate bowl. Season to taste with salt and pepper. Cover and set aside in the refrigerator until required.

3 Add the tomatoes to the garlic mixture, discarding the drained juice.

4 Bring a large pan of lightly salted water to a boil. Add the fettuccine, return to a boil, and cook for 8–10 minutes, or until tender but still firm to the bite. Drain, then tip into a warmed serving bowl. Add the garlic and tomato mixture and toss well. Serve immediately.

spaghetti olio e aglio

ingredients

serves 4

1 lb/450 g dried spaghetti
½ cup extra virgin olive oil
3 garlic cloves, finely chopped
salt and pepper
3 tbsp chopped fresh flat-leaf parsley

method

1. Bring a large, heavy-bottom pan of lightly salted water to a boil. Add the spaghetti, return to a boil, and cook the pasta for 8–10 minutes, or until tender but still firm to the bite.
2. Meanwhile, heat the olive oil in a heavy-bottom skillet. Add the garlic and a pinch of salt and cook over low heat, stirring continuously, for 3–4 minutes, or until golden. Do not allow the garlic to brown or it will taste bitter. Remove the skillet from the heat.
3. Drain the pasta and transfer to a warmed serving dish. Pour in the garlic-flavored olive oil, then add the chopped parsley and season with salt and pepper. Toss well and serve immediately.

farfalle with cream & cheese

ingredients

serves 4

1 lb/450 g dried farfalle
2 tbsp unsalted butter
12 oz/350 g/3 cups baby peas
7 fl oz/200 ml/generous ¾ cup heavy cream
pinch of freshly grated nutmeg
2 oz/55 g/½ cup freshly grated Parmesan cheese, plus extra to serve
salt and pepper
fresh flat-leaf parsley sprigs, to garnish
crusty bread, to serve

method

1 Bring a large pan of lightly salted water to a boil. Add the pasta, return to a boil, and cook for 8–10 minutes, or until tender but still firm to the bite, then drain the pasta thoroughly.

2 Melt the butter in a large, heavy-bottom pan. Add the baby peas and cook for 2–3 minutes. Add 5 fl oz/ 150 ml/⅔ cup of the cream and bring to a boil. Reduce the heat and simmer for 1 minute, or until slightly thickened.

3 Add the drained pasta to the cream mixture. Place the pan over low heat and toss until the farfalle are thoroughly coated. Season with nutmeg, salt and pepper, then add the remaining cream and the grated Parmesan cheese. Toss again and transfer to individual serving bowls. Garnish with parsley sprigs and serve immediately with extra Parmesan cheese, for sprinkling, and crusty bread.

fettuccine with bell peppers & olives

ingredients

serves 4

- ⅓ cup olive oil
- 1 onion, finely chopped
- 7 oz/200 g/1 cup black olives, pitted and coarsely chopped
- 14 oz/400 g canned chopped tomatoes, drained
- 2 red, yellow, or orange bell peppers, seeded and cut into thin strips
- 12 oz/350 g dried fettuccine
- salt and pepper
- shavings of Romano cheese, to serve

method

1. Heat the oil in a large heavy-bottom pan. Add the onion and cook over low heat, stirring occasionally, for 5 minutes, or until softened. Add the olives, tomatoes, and bell peppers, and season to taste with salt and pepper. Cover and let simmer gently over very low heat, stirring occasionally, for 35 minutes.

2. Meanwhile, bring a large heavy-bottom pan of lightly salted water to a boil. Add the pasta, return to a boil, and cook for 8–10 minutes, or until tender but still firm to the bite. Drain the pasta and transfer to a warmed serving dish.

3. Spoon the sauce onto the pasta and toss well. Sprinkle generously with the Romano cheese and serve immediately.

pipe rigate with gorgonzola sauce

ingredients

serves 4

14 oz/400 g dried pipe rigate, rigatoni, or penne
2 tbsp unsalted butter
6 fresh sage leaves
7 oz/200 g Gorgonzola cheese, diced
6–8 fl oz/175–225 ml/ 3/4–1 cup heavy cream
2 tbsp dry vermouth
salt and pepper

method

1 Bring a large heavy-bottom pan of lightly salted water to a boil. Add the pasta, return to a boil, and cook for 8–10 minutes, until tender but still firm to the bite.

2 Meanwhile, melt the butter in a separate heavy-bottom pan. Add the sage leaves and cook, stirring gently, for 1 minute. Remove and reserve the sage leaves. Add the cheese and cook, stirring constantly, over low heat until it has melted. Gradually, stir in 6 fl oz/ 175 ml/3/4 cup of the cream and the vermouth. Season with salt and pepper and cook, stirring, until thickened. Add more cream if the sauce seems too thick.

3 Drain the pasta well and transfer to a warmed serving dish. Add the Gorgonzola sauce, toss well to mix, and serve at once, garnished with the reserved sage leaves.

pasta with green vegetables

ingredients

serves 4

8 oz/225 g dried gemelli or other pasta shapes
2 tbsp chopped fresh parsley
2 tbsp freshly grated Parmesan cheese

sauce

1 head of broccoli, cut into florets
2 zucchini, sliced
8 oz/225 g asparagus, trimmed
4½ oz/125 g snow peas
4½ oz/125 g frozen peas
2 tbsp butter
3 tbsp vegetable stock
5 tbsp heavy cream
salt and pepper
large pinch of freshly grated nutmeg

method

1 Bring a large, heavy-bottom pan of lightly salted water to a boil. Add the pasta, return to a boil, and cook for 8–10 minutes, or until the pasta is tender but still firm to the bite. Drain the pasta, return to the pan, cover, and keep warm.

2 Steam the broccoli, zucchini, asparagus, and snow peas over a pan of boiling, salted water until just beginning to soften. Remove from the heat and plunge into cold water to prevent further cooking. Drain and reserve. Cook the peas in boiling, salted water for 3 minutes, then drain. Refresh in cold water and drain again.

3 Place the butter and vegetable stock in a pan over medium heat. Add all the vegetables except for the asparagus and toss carefully with a wooden spoon to heat through, taking care not to break them up. Stir in the cream, let the sauce heat through, and season with salt, pepper, and nutmeg.

4 Transfer the pasta to a warmed serving dish and stir in the chopped parsley. Spoon the sauce over, and sprinkle on the freshly grated Parmesan cheese. Arrange the asparagus in a pattern on top. Serve immediately.

spaghetti alla norma

ingredients

serves 4

¾ cup olive oil
1 lb 2 oz/500 g plum tomatoes, peeled and chopped
1 garlic clove, chopped
12 oz/350 g eggplant, diced
14 oz/400 g dried spaghetti
½ bunch fresh basil, torn
4 oz/115 g/1⅓ cups freshly grated Romano cheese
salt and pepper

method

1 Heat 4 tablespoons of the oil in a large pan. Add the tomatoes and garlic, season to taste with salt and pepper, cover, and cook over low heat, stirring occasionally, for 25 minutes.

2 Meanwhile, heat the remaining oil in a heavy skillet. Add the eggplant and cook, stirring occasionally, for 5 minutes, until evenly golden brown. Remove with a slotted spoon and drain on paper towels.

3 Bring a large pan of lightly salted water to a boil. Add the pasta, bring back to a boil, and cook for 8–10 minutes, until tender but still firm to the bite.

4 Meanwhile, stir the drained eggplant into the pan of tomatoes. Taste and adjust the seasoning, if necessary.

5 Drain the pasta and place in a warmed serving dish. Add the tomato and eggplant mixture, basil, and half the Romano cheese. Toss well, sprinkle with the remaining cheese, and serve immediately.

pappardelle with pumpkin sauce

ingredients

serves 4

4 tbsp butter
6 shallots, very finely chopped
1 lb 12 oz/800 g pumpkin, peeled, seeded, and cut into pieces
pinch of freshly grated nutmeg
7 fl oz/200 ml/¾ cup light cream
4 tbsp freshly grated Parmesan cheese, plus extra to serve
2 tbsp chopped fresh flat-leaf parsley
12 oz/350 g dried pappardelle
salt

method

1 Melt the butter in a large, heavy-bottom pan. Add the shallots, sprinkle with a little salt, cover, and cook over very low heat, stirring occasionally, for 30 minutes.

2 Add the pumpkin pieces and season to taste with nutmeg. Cover and cook over very low heat, stirring occasionally, for 40 minutes, or until the pumpkin is pulpy. Stir in the cream, Parmesan cheese, and parsley, and remove the pan from the heat.

3 Meanwhile, bring a large, heavy-bottom pan of lightly salted water to a boil. Add the pasta, return to a boil, and cook for 8–10 minutes, or until tender but still firm to the bite. Drain, reserving 2–3 tablespoons of the cooking water.

4 Add the pasta to the pumpkin mixture and stir in the reserved cooking water if the mixture seems too thick. Cook, stirring constantly, for 1 minute, then transfer to a warmed serving dish and serve immediately with extra grated Parmesan cheese.

tagliatelle with asparagus & gorgonzola sauce

ingredients

serves 4

1 lb/450 g asparagus tips
1 tbsp olive oil
8 oz/225 g Gorgonzola, crumbled
6 fl oz/175 ml/¾ cup heavy cream
12 oz/350 g dried tagliatelle
salt and pepper

method

1 Place the asparagus tips in a single layer in a shallow ovenproof dish. Sprinkle with a little olive oil and season with salt and pepper. Turn to coat in the oil and seasoning. Roast in a preheated oven, 450°F/230°C, for 10–12 minutes until slightly browned and just tender. Set aside and keep warm.

2 Combine the crumbled cheese with the cream in a bowl. Season with salt and pepper.

3 Cook the pasta in plenty of boiling salted water until tender but still firm to the bite. Drain and transfer to a warmed serving dish.

4 Immediately add the asparagus and the cheese mixture. Toss well until the cheese has melted and the pasta is coated with the sauce. Serve at once.

pasta with spiced leek, butternut squash & cherry tomatoes

ingredients

serves 4

5½oz/150 g baby leeks, cut into ¾-inch/2-cm slices
6 oz/175 g butternut squash, seeded and cut into ¾-inch/2-cm chunks
1½ tbsp medium curry paste
1 tsp vegetable oil
6 oz/175 g cherry tomatoes
9 oz/250 g dried pasta shapes
2 tbsp chopped fresh cilantro leaves

white sauce

9 fl oz/250 ml/generous 1 cup skim milk
¾ oz/20 g cornstarch
1 tsp mustard powder
1 small onion, left whole
2 small bay leaves
4 tsp grated Parmesan cheese

method

1 To make the white sauce, put the milk into a small pan with the cornstarch, mustard, onion, and bay leaves. Whisk over medium heat until thick. Remove from the heat, discard the onion and bay leaves, and stir in the cheese. Set aside, stirring occasionally.

2 Bring a large pan of water to a boil, add the leeks and cook for 2 minutes. Add the butternut squash and cook for a further 2 minutes. Drain in a colander.

3 Mix the curry paste with the oil in a large bowl. Toss the leeks and butternut squash in the mixture to coat thoroughly.

4 Transfer the leeks and butternut squash to a nonstick cookie sheet and roast in a preheated oven, 400°F/200°C, for 10 minutes until golden brown. Add the tomatoes and roast for a further 5 minutes.

5 Meanwhile, cook the pasta in a large pan according to the instructions on the package and drain.

6 Put the white sauce into a large pan and warm over low heat. Add the leeks, butternut squash, tomatoes, and cilantro and stir in the warm pasta. Mix thoroughly and serve.

spaghetti with tomato, garlic & basil sauce

ingredients

serves 4

5 tbsp extra virgin olive oil
1 onion, finely chopped
1 lb 12 oz/800 g canned chopped tomatoes
4 garlic cloves, cut into fourths
1 lb/450 g dried spaghetti
large handful fresh basil leaves, shredded
salt and pepper
fresh Parmesan cheese shavings, to serve

method

1 Heat the oil in a large pan over medium heat. Add the onion and fry gently for 5 minutes until soft. Add the tomatoes and garlic. Bring to a boil, then let simmer over medium-low heat for 25–30 minutes until the oil separates from the tomato. Season with salt and pepper.

2 Cook the pasta in plenty of boiling salted water until tender but still firm to the bite. Drain and transfer to a warmed serving dish.

3 Pour the sauce over the pasta. Add the basil and toss well to mix. Serve with the Parmesan cheese shavings.

fusilli with herbed sun-dried tomato sauce

ingredients

serves 4

3 oz/85 g sun-dried tomatoes (not in oil)
24 fl oz/750 ml/3 cups boiling water
2 tbsp olive oil
1 onion, finely chopped
2 large garlic cloves, finely sliced
2 tbsp chopped fresh flat-leaf parsley
2 tsp chopped fresh oregano
1 tsp chopped fresh rosemary
12 oz/350 g dried fusilli
salt and pepper
10 fresh basil leaves, shredded and 3 tbsp freshly grated Parmesan cheese, to serve

method

1 Put the tomatoes and boiling water in a bowl and let stand for 5 minutes. Using a perforated spoon, remove one third of the tomatoes from the bowl. Cut into bite-size pieces. Put the remaining tomatoes and water into a blender and puree.

2 Heat the oil in a large skillet over medium heat. Add the onion and gently fry for 5 minutes until soft. Add the garlic and fry until just beginning to color. Add the pureed tomato and the reserved tomato pieces to the pan. Bring to a boil, then let simmer over medium-low heat for 10 minutes. Stir in the herbs and season with salt and pepper. Let simmer for 1 minute, then remove from the heat.

3 Cook the pasta in plenty of boiling salted water, until tender but still firm to the bite. Drain and transfer to a warmed serving dish. Briefly reheat the sauce. Pour over the pasta, add the basil and toss well to mix. Sprinkle with the Parmesan cheese and serve immediately.

penne in a creamy mushroom sauce

ingredients

serves 4

- 4 tbsp butter
- 1 tbsp olive oil
- 6 shallots, sliced
- 1 lb/450 g chestnut mushrooms, sliced
- 1 tsp plain flour
- 5 fl oz/150 ml/⅔ cup heavy cream
- 2 tbsp port
- 4 oz/115 g sun-dried tomatoes in oil, drained and chopped
- pinch freshly grated nutmeg
- 12 oz/350 g dried penne
- salt and pepper
- 2 tbsp chopped fresh flat-leaf parsley

method

1. Melt the butter with the olive oil in a large, heavy-bottom skillet. Add the shallots and cook over low heat, stirring occasionally, for 4–5 minutes, or until softened. Add the mushrooms and cook over low heat for a further 2 minutes. Season with salt and pepper, sprinkle in the flour and cook, stirring, for 1 minute.
2. Remove the skillet from the heat and gradually stir in the cream and port. Return to the heat, add the sun-dried tomatoes and grated nutmeg, and cook over low heat, stirring occasionally, for 8 minutes.
3. Meanwhile, bring a large, heavy-bottom pan of lightly salted water to a boil. Add the pasta, return to a boil and cook for 8–10 minutes, or until tender but still firm to the bite. Drain the pasta well and add to the mushroom sauce. Cook for 3 minutes, then transfer to a warmed serving dish. Sprinkle with the chopped parsley and serve immediately.

fusilli with gorgonzola & mushroom sauce

ingredients

serves 4

12 oz/350 g dried fusilli
3 tbsp olive oil
12 oz/350 g wild mushrooms or white mushrooms, sliced
1 garlic clove, finely chopped
14 fl oz/400 ml/1¾ cups heavy cream
9 oz/250 g Gorgonzola cheese, crumbled
salt and pepper
2 tbsp chopped fresh flat-leaf parsley, to garnish

method

1 Bring a large pan of lightly salted water to a boil. Add the pasta, return to a boil, and cook for 8–10 minutes, or until tender but still firm to the bite.

2 Meanwhile, heat the olive oil in a heavy-bottom pan. Add the mushrooms and cook over low heat, stirring frequently, for 5 minutes. Add the garlic to the pan and cook for an additional 2 minutes.

3 Add the cream, bring to a boil, and cook for 1 minute, until slightly thickened. Stir in the cheese and cook over low heat until it has melted. Do not allow the sauce to boil once the cheese has been added. Season with salt and pepper and remove the pan from the heat.

4 Drain the pasta and tip it into the sauce. Toss well to coat, then serve immediately, garnished with the parsley.

tagliatelle with roasted artichokes & horseradish-herb sauce

ingredients

serves 2

- 3½ oz/100 g canned artichokes, cut into quarters
- vegetable oil spray
- 1¾ oz/50 g fresh baby spinach leaves, washed
- 3½ oz/100 g dried tagliatelle
- 3½ oz/100 ml white sauce (see page 144)
- 2 tsp chopped fresh basil, plus extra to garnish
- 1 tsp finely chopped fresh lemon thyme, plus extra to garnish
- 1 tsp creamed horseradish
- 2 tsp sour cream

method

1. Spread the artichokes out on a nonstick cookie sheet, spray lightly with oil, and roast in a preheated oven, 425°F/220°C, for 20 minutes until golden brown.
2. Meanwhile, heat a large, lidded pan over medium heat. Add the spinach, cover, and steam for 2 minutes. Remove from the heat and drain the spinach in a colander.
3. Cook the pasta according to the instructions on the package and drain.
4. Return the drained spinach to the pan. Make the white sauce and heat gently. Add the herbs, horseradish, sour cream, and artichokes and stir in the warm pasta. Heat to warm through, then serve garnished with extra herbs.

conchiglie with marinated artichoke, onion & tomato sauce

ingredients

serves 4

- 10 oz/280 g bottled marinated artichoke hearts
- 3 tbsp olive oil
- 1 onion, finely chopped
- 3 garlic cloves, minced
- 1 tsp dried oregano
- ¼ tsp dried chile flakes
- 14 oz/400 g canned chopped tomatoes
- 12 oz/350 g dried conchiglie
- 4 tsp freshly grated Parmesan cheese
- 3 tbsp chopped fresh flat-leaf parsley
- salt and pepper

method

1. Drain the artichoke hearts, reserving the marinade. Heat the oil in a large pan over medium heat. Add the onion and fry for 5 minutes until translucent. Add the garlic, oregano, chile flakes, and the reserved artichoke marinade. Cook for an additional 5 minutes.

2. Stir in the tomatoes. Bring to a boil, then simmer over medium-low heat for 30 minutes. Season generously with salt and pepper.

3. Cook the pasta in plenty of boiling salted water until tender but still firm to the bite. Drain and transfer to a warmed serving dish.

4. Add the artichokes, Parmesan cheese, and parsley to the sauce. Cook for a few minutes until heated through. Pour the sauce over the pasta, toss well to mix, and serve at once.

fusilli with zucchini, lemon & rosemary sauce

ingredients

serves 4

6 tbsp olive oil
1 small onion, very thinly sliced
2 garlic cloves, very finely chopped
2 tbsp chopped fresh rosemary
1 tbsp chopped fresh flat-leaf parsley
1 lb/450 g small zucchini, cut into ¼-inch x 1½-inch/5-mm x 4-cm strips
finely grated rind of 1 lemon
1 lb/450 g fusilli tricolore
salt and pepper
4 tbsp freshly grated Parmesan cheese

method

1 Heat the olive oil in a large skillet over medium-low heat. Add the onion and gently fry, stirring occasionally, for about 10 minutes until golden.

2 Raise the heat to medium-high. Add the garlic, rosemary, and parsley and cook for a few seconds, stirring. Add the zucchini and lemon rind. Cook for 5–7 minutes, stirring occasionally, until the zucchini are just tender. Season with salt and pepper. Remove from the heat.

3 Cook the pasta in plenty of boiling salted water until tender but still firm to the bite. Drain and transfer to a warmed serving dish.

4 Briefly reheat the zucchini. Pour over the pasta and toss well to mix. Sprinkle with the Parmesan cheese and serve immediately.

tagliatelle with walnuts

ingredients

serves 4

- 1 oz/25 g/½ cup fresh white bread crumbs
- 12 oz/350 g/3 cups walnut pieces, plus extra to garnish
- 2 garlic cloves, finely chopped
- 4 tbsp milk
- 4 tbsp olive oil
- 3 oz/85 g/⅜ cup cream cheese
- 5 fl oz/150 ml/⅔ cup light cream
- 12 oz/350 g dried tagliatelle
- salt and pepper

method

1. Place the bread crumbs, walnuts, garlic, milk, olive oil, and cream cheese in a large mortar and grind to a smooth paste with a pestle. Alternatively, place the ingredients in a food processor and process until smooth. Stir in the cream to give a thick sauce consistency and season with salt and pepper. Set aside.
2. Bring a large heavy-bottom pan of lightly salted water to a boil. Add the pasta, return to a boil, and cook for 8–10 minutes, or until tender but still firm to the bite.
3. Drain the pasta and transfer to a warmed serving dish. Add the walnut sauce and toss thoroughly to coat. Sprinkle with extra chopped walnuts and serve immediately.

tagliatelle with wild mushrooms & mascarpone

ingredients

serves 4

1 lb/450 g dried tagliatelle
4 tbsp butter
1 garlic clove, crushed
8 oz/225 g mixed wild mushrooms, sliced
generous 1 cup Mascarpone cheese
2 tbsp milk
1 tsp chopped fresh sage
salt and pepper
freshly grated Parmesan cheese, to serve

method

1. Bring a large, heavy-bottom saucepan of lightly salted water to a boil. Add the pasta, return to a boil and cook for 8–10 minutes, or until tender but still firm to the bite.

2. Meanwhile, melt the butter in a separate large pan. Add the garlic and mushrooms and cook for 3–4 minutes.

3. Reduce the heat and stir in the Mascarpone cheese, milk, and sage. Season to taste with salt and pepper.

4. Drain the pasta thoroughly and add to the mushroom sauce. Toss until the pasta is well coated with the sauce. Transfer the pasta to warmed dishes and serve immediately with Parmesan cheese.

ziti with arugula

ingredients

serves 4

12 oz/350 g dried ziti, broken into 1½-inch/4-cm lengths
5 tbsp extra virgin olive oil
2 garlic cloves, lightly crushed
7 oz/200 g arugula
2 fresh red chiles, thickly sliced
fresh red chile flowers, to garnish
freshly grated romano cheese, to serve

method

1 Bring a large, heavy-bottom pan of lightly salted water to a boil. Add the pasta, return to a boil, and cook for 8–10 minutes, or until tender but still firm to the bite.

2 Meanwhile, heat the olive oil in a large, heavy-bottom skillet. Add the garlic, arugula, and chiles and stir-fry for 5 minutes, or until the arugula has wilted.

3 Stir 2 tablespoons of the pasta cooking water into the arugula, then drain the pasta and add to the skillet. Cook, stirring frequently, for 2 minutes, then transfer to a warmed serving dish. Remove and discard the garlic cloves and chiles, garnish with red chile flowers, and serve immediately with the romano cheese.

variation

For a subtler, less peppery taste, replace the arugula with 7 oz/200 g baby spinach instead.

linguine with roasted garlic & red bell pepper sauce

ingredients

serves 4

- 6 large garlic cloves, unpeeled
- 14 oz/400 g bottled roasted red bell peppers, strained and sliced
- 7 oz/200 g canned chopped tomatoes
- 3 tbsp olive oil
- 1/4 tsp dried chile flakes
- 1 tsp chopped fresh thyme or oregano
- 12 oz/350 g dried linguine, spaghetti, or bucatini
- salt and pepper
- freshly grated Parmesan cheese, to serve

method

1. Place the unpeeled garlic cloves in a shallow, ovenproof dish. Roast in a preheated oven at 400°F/200°C for 7–10 minutes until the cloves feel soft.

2. Put the bell peppers, tomatoes, and oil in a food processor or blender, then puree. Squeeze the garlic flesh into the puree. Add the chile flakes and thyme. Season with salt and pepper. Blend again, then scrape into a pan and set aside.

3. Cook the pasta in plenty of boiling salted water until tender but still firm to the bite. Drain and transfer to a warmed serving dish.

4. Reheat the sauce and pour over the pasta. Toss well to mix. Serve at once with Parmesan cheese.

vegetable ravioli

ingredients

serves 4

2 large eggplants, cut into 1-inch/2.5-cm chunks
6 large tomatoes
½ cup olive oil
3 garlic cloves, chopped
1 large onion, chopped
3 large zucchini cut into chunks
1 large green and 1 large red bell pepper, seeded and cut into chunks
4½ tsp tomato paste
½ tsp chopped fresh basil, plus extra sprigs to garnish
basic pasta dough (see page 14)
all-purpose flour, for dusting
6 tbsp butter
⅔ cup light cream
¾ cup freshly grated Parmesan cheese
salt and pepper

method

1 To make the filling, place the eggplant pieces in a colander, sprinkle with salt, and let stand for 20 minutes. Rinse and drain, then pat dry on paper towels.

2 Blanch the tomatoes in boiling water for 2 minutes. Drain, peel, and chop the flesh. Heat the oil in a large pan over low heat. Add the garlic and onion and cook for 3 minutes. Stir in the eggplants, zucchini, tomatoes, bell peppers, tomato paste, and chopped basil. Season to taste. Cover, and simmer for 20 minutes.

3 Roll out the pasta dough on a lightly floured surface to a thin rectangle about the thickness of a nickel. Using a 2-inch/5-cm plain cookie cutter, stamp out rounds.

4 Place small mounds, about 1 teaspoon each, of the filling on half of the rounds. Brush the edges with a little water, then cover with the remaining rounds, pressing the edges to seal. Place on a dish towel and let stand for 1 hour. Preheat the oven to 400°F/200°C. Bring a large pan of lightly salted water to a boil over medium heat. Add the ravioli and cook for about 3–4 minutes. Drain and transfer to a greased ovenproof dish, dotting each layer with butter. Pour over the cream and sprinkle over the Parmesan. Bake in the preheated oven for 20 minutes. Garnish with basil sprigs and serve.

garlic mushroom ravioli

ingredients

serves 4

5½ tbsp butter
50 g/1¾ oz/⅓ cup finely chopped shallots
3 garlic cloves, crushed
50 g/1¾ oz/¾ cup finely chopped mushrooms
½ celery stalk, finely chopped
1 oz/25 g/¼ cup finely grated pecorino cheese, plus extra to garnish
basic pasta dough (see page 14)
all-purpose flour, for dusting
1 egg, lightly beaten
salt and pepper

method

1 Heat 2 tablespoons of the butter in a skillet. Add the shallots, 1 crushed garlic clove, the mushrooms, and celery and cook for 4–5 minutes. Remove the skillet from the heat, stir in the pecorino cheese, and season to taste. Using a ½ quantity of pasta dough, divide the pasta dough in half and wrap 1 piece in clingfilm.

2 Roll out the other piece on a lightly floured surface to a thin rectangle about the thickness of a nickel. Cover with a damp dish towel and roll out the other piece of dough to the same size. Place small mounds, about 1 teaspoon each, of the filling in rows about 1½ inches/4 cm apart on a sheet of pasta dough. Brush the spaces between the mounds with the beaten egg. Lift the second sheet of dough on top of the first and press down firmly between the pockets of filling, pushing out any air bubbles. Using a pasta wheel or sharp knife, cut into squares. Place on a dish towel and let stand for 1 hour. Bring a heavy-bottom saucepan of water to a boil, add the ravioli, and cook in batches for 2–3 minutes. Remove with a slotted spoon and drain.

3 Meanwhile, melt the remaining butter in a skillet, then add the remaining garlic and plenty of pepper and cook for 1–2 minutes. Transfer the ravioli to plates and pour over the garlic butter. Garnish with the pecorino cheese and serve immediately.

spinach & ricotta ravioli

ingredients

serves 4

spinach pasta dough

8 oz/225 g spinach leaves
7 oz/200 g/1 cup all-purpose flour, plus extra for dusting
pinch of salt
2 eggs, lightly beaten
1 tbsp olive oil

filling

12 oz/350 g spinach leaves, coarse stalks removed
8 oz/225 g/1 cup ricotta cheese
2 oz/55 g/½ cup freshly grated Parmesan cheese, plus extra, to serve
2 eggs, lightly beaten
pinch of freshly grated nutmeg
pepper
all-purpose flour, for dusting

method

1 To make the pasta dough, blanch the spinach in boiling water for 1 minute. Drain thoroughly and chop finely. Sift the flour into a food processor. Add the spinach, salt, eggs, and olive oil and process until the dough begins to come together. Knead on a lightly floured counter until smooth. Cover and let rest for 30 minutes.

2 To make the filling, cook the spinach, with just the water clinging to the leaves after washing, over low heat for 5 minutes, or until wilted. Drain and squeeze out as much moisture as possible. Cool, then chop finely. Beat the ricotta cheese until smooth, then stir in the spinach, Parmesan cheese, and half the egg, and season with nutmeg and pepper.

3 Halve the pasta dough. Roll out one half on a floured counter. Cover, and roll out the other half. Put small mounds of filling in rows 1½ inches/4 cm apart on one sheet of dough and brush in between with the remaining egg. Cover with the other half. Press down between the mounds, pushing out any air. Cut into squares and let rest on a dish towel for 1 hour.

4 Bring a large pan of salted water to a boil, add the ravioli, in batches, return to a boil, and cook for 5 minutes. Remove with a slotted spoon and drain on paper towels. Serve with grated Parmesan cheese.

al forno

lasagna

ingredients

serves 4

3 tbsp olive oil
1 onion, finely chopped
1 celery stalk, finely chopped
1 carrot, finely chopped
3½ oz/100 g pancetta or rindless lean bacon, finely chopped
6 oz/175 g ground beef
6 oz/175 g ground pork
3 fl oz/90 ml/⅓ cup dry red wine
5 fl oz/150 ml/⅔ cup beef stock
1 tbsp tomato paste
1 clove
1 bay leaf
5 fl oz/150 ml/⅔ cup boiling milk
4 tbsp unsalted butter, diced, plus extra for greasing
14 oz/400 g dried lasagna
béchamel sauce (see below)
5 oz/140 g mozzarella cheese
5 oz/140 g/1¼ cups freshly grated Parmesan cheese

basic béchamel sauce

2 tbsp butter
1 tbsp plain flour
12 fl oz/350 ml warm milk
salt and pepper

method

1 Heat the olive oil in a large, heavy-bottom pan. Add the onion, celery, carrot, pancetta, beef, and pork and cook over medium heat, stirring frequently for 10 minutes, or until lightly browned.

2 Add the wine, stock, and tomato paste to the pan, boil and reduce. Season with salt and pepper, add the clove and bay leaf, and pour in the milk. Cover and let simmer over low heat for 1½ hours. Remove from the heat and discard the clove and bay leaf.

3 To make the béchamel sauce, melt the butter in a pan over a low heat. Add the flour and stir with a wooden spoon. Turn the heat up a little and continue stirring for 2 minutes. Add half of the milk and stir to make a smooth paste. Add the remaining milk, stirring until you have a smooth, white sauce. Season.

4 Lightly grease a large, ovenproof dish with butter. Place a layer of lasagna in the bottom and cover it with a layer of meat sauce. Spoon a layer of béchamel sauce on top and sprinkle with one third of the cheese. Make layers until all the ingredients are used, ending with a topping of béchamel sauce and sprinkled cheese.

5 Dot the top of the lasagna with the diced butter and bake in a preheated oven, 400°F/200°C, for 30 minutes, or until golden and bubbling.

marsala mushroom lasagna

ingredients

serves 4

béchamel sauce (see page 176)
butter, for greasing
14 sheets dried no-precook lasagna
3 oz/75 g/¾ cup grated Parmesan cheese

mushroom sauce

2 tbsp olive oil
2 garlic cloves, crushed
1 large onion, finely chopped
8 oz/225 g exotic mushrooms, sliced
10½ oz/300 g/generous 1¼ cups fresh ground chicken
3 oz/75 g chicken livers, finely chopped
4 oz/115 g prosciutto, diced
5 fl oz/150 ml/⅔ cup Marsala wine
10 oz/285 g canned chopped tomatoes
1 tbsp chopped fresh basil leaves
2 tbsp tomato paste
salt and pepper

method

1. To make the mushroom sauce, heat the olive oil in a large, heavy-bottom pan. Add the garlic, onion, and mushrooms, and cook, stirring frequently, for 6 minutes. Add the ground chicken, chicken livers, and prosciutto, and cook over low heat for 12 minutes, or until the meat has browned.

2. Stir the Marsala, tomatoes, basil, and tomato paste into the mixture, and cook for 4 minutes. Season with salt and pepper, cover, and let simmer for 30 minutes. Uncover, stir, then let simmer for an additional 15 minutes.

3. Make a triple quantity of béchamel sauce.

4. Lightly grease an ovenproof dish with butter. Arrange sheets of lasagna over the base of the dish, spoon over a layer of the mushroom sauce, then spoon over a layer of béchamel sauce. Place another layer of lasagna on top and repeat the process twice, finishing with a layer of béchamel sauce. Sprinkle over the grated cheese and bake in a preheated oven, 375°F/190°C, for 35 minutes, or until golden brown and bubbling. Serve immediately.

pasticcio

ingredients

serves 4

1 tbsp olive oil
1 onion, chopped
2 garlic cloves, finely chopped
1 lb/450 g/2 cups fresh ground lamb
2 tbsp tomato paste
2 tbsp all-purpose flour
10 fl oz/300 ml/1¼ cups chicken stock
1 tsp ground cinnamon
4 oz/115 g dried short-cut macaroni
2 beefsteak tomatoes, sliced
10 fl oz/300 ml/1¼ cups strained plain yogurt
2 eggs, lightly beaten
salt and pepper

method

1. Heat the olive oil in a large heavy-bottom skillet. Add the onion and garlic and cook over low heat, stirring occasionally, for 5 minutes, or until softened. Add the lamb and cook, breaking it up with a wooden spoon, until browned all over. Add the tomato paste and sprinkle in the flour. Cook, stirring, for 1 minute, then stir in the chicken stock. Season with salt and pepper and stir in the cinnamon. Bring to a boil, reduce the heat, cover, and cook for 25 minutes.

2. Meanwhile, bring a large heavy-bottom pan of lightly salted water to a boil. Add the pasta, return to a boil, and cook for 8–10 minutes, or until tender but still firm to the bite.

3. Spoon the lamb mixture into a large ovenproof dish and arrange the tomato slices on top. Drain the pasta and transfer to a bowl. Add the yogurt and eggs and mix well. Spoon the pasta mixture on top of the lamb and bake in a preheated oven, 375°F/190°C, for 1 hour. Serve immediately.

cannelloni with ham & ricotta

ingredients

serves 4

2 tbsp olive oil
2 onions, chopped
2 garlic cloves, finely chopped
1 tbsp shredded fresh basil
1 lb 12 oz/800 g chopped tomatoes
1 tbsp tomato paste
12 oz/350 g dried cannelloni tubes
butter, for greasing
8 oz/225 g/1 cup ricotta cheese
4 oz/115 g cooked ham, diced
1 egg
2 oz/55 g/½ cup freshly grated romano cheese
salt and pepper

method

1 Heat the olive oil in a large, heavy-bottom skillet. Add the onions and garlic and cook over low heat, stirring occasionally, for 5 minutes, or until the onion is softened. Add the basil, chopped tomatoes and their can juices, and tomato paste and season with salt and pepper. Reduce the heat and let simmer for 30 minutes, or until thickened.

2 Meanwhile, bring a large, heavy-bottom pan of lightly salted water to a boil. Add the dried cannelloni tubes, return to a boil, and cook for 8–10 minutes, or until tender but still firm to the bite. Using a slotted spoon, transfer the cannelloni tubes to a large plate and pat dry with paper towels.

3 Grease a large, shallow ovenproof dish with butter. Mix the ricotta, ham, and egg together in a bowl and season with salt and pepper. Using a teaspoon, fill the cannelloni tubes with the ricotta, ham, and egg mixture and place in a single layer in the dish. Pour the tomato sauce over the cannelloni and sprinkle with the grated romano cheese. Bake in a preheated oven, 350°F/180°C, for 30 minutes, or until golden brown. Serve at once.

chicken lasagna

ingredients

serves 6

2 tbsp olive oil
2 lb/900 g/4 cups fresh ground chicken
1 garlic clove, finely chopped
4 carrots, chopped
4 leeks, sliced
16 fl oz/450 ml/2 cups chicken stock
2 tbsp tomato paste
béchamel sauce (see page 176)
4 oz/115 g Cheddar cheese, grated
1 tsp Dijon mustard
4 oz/115 g dried no-precook lasagna
salt and pepper

method

1 Heat the oil in a heavy-bottom pan. Add the chicken and cook over medium heat, breaking it up with a wooden spoon, for 5 minutes, or until it is browned all over. Add the garlic, carrots, and leeks to the pan, and cook, stirring occasionally, for 5 minutes.

2 Stir in the chicken stock and tomato paste and season with salt and pepper. Bring to a boil, reduce the heat, cover, and let simmer for 30 minutes.

3 Make a double quantity of béchamel sauce.

4 Whisk half the cheese and the mustard into the hot béchamel sauce. In a large ovenproof dish, make alternate layers of the chicken mixture, lasagna, and cheese sauce, ending with a layer of cheese sauce. Sprinkle with the remaining cheese and bake in a preheated oven, 375°F/190°C, for 1 hour, or until golden brown and bubbling. Serve at once.

chicken & wild mushroom cannelloni

ingredients

serves 4

butter, for greasing
2 tbsp olive oil
2 garlic cloves, crushed
1 large onion, finely chopped
8 oz/225 g wild mushrooms, sliced
12 oz/350 g ground chicken
115 g/4 oz prosciutto, diced
5 fl oz/150 ml/⅔ cup Marsala wine
7 oz/200 g canned chopped tomatoes
1 tbsp shredded fresh basil leaves
2 tbsp tomato paste
10–12 dried cannelloni tubes
béchamel sauce (see page 176)
3 oz/85 g/¾ cup freshly grated Parmesan cheese
salt and pepper

method

1 Lightly grease a large ovenproof dish. Heat the olive oil in a heavy-bottom skillet. Add the garlic, onion, and mushrooms and cook over low heat, stirring frequently, for 8–10 minutes. Add the ground chicken and prosciutto and cook, stirring frequently, until browned all over. Stir in the Marsala, tomatoes and their can juices, basil, and tomato paste and cook for 4 minutes. Season with salt and pepper, then cover and simmer for 30 minutes. Uncover, stir, and simmer for 15 minutes.

2 Meanwhile, bring a large, heavy-bottom pan of lightly salted water to a boil. Add the pasta, return to a boil, and cook for 8–10 minutes, or until tender but still firm to the bite. Using a slotted spoon, transfer the pasta to a plate and pat dry with paper towels.

3 Make a double quantity of béchamel sauce.

4 Fill the cannelloni tubes with the chicken, prosciutto, and mushroom mixture. Transfer them to the ovenproof dish. Pour the béchamel sauce over them to cover completely and sprinkle with the grated Parmesan cheese. Bake the cannelloni in a preheated oven, 375°F/190°C, for 30 minutes, or until golden brown and bubbling. Serve immediately.

lasagna alla marinara

ingredients

serves 6

1 tbsp butter
8 oz/225 g raw shrimp, shelled, deveined, and coarsely chopped
1 lb/450 g monkfish fillets, skinned and chopped
8 oz/225 g cremini mushrooms, chopped
béchamel sauce (see page 176)
14 oz/400 g canned chopped tomatoes
1 tbsp chopped fresh chervil
1 tbsp shredded fresh basil
6 oz/175 g dried no-precook lasagna
3 oz/85 g/¾ cup freshly grated Parmesan cheese
salt and pepper

method

1 Melt the butter in a large, heavy-bottom pan. Add the shrimp and monkfish and cook over medium heat for 3–5 minutes, or until the shrimp change color. Transfer the shrimp to a small heatproof bowl with a slotted spoon. Add the mushrooms to the pan and cook, stirring occasionally, for 5 minutes. Transfer the fish and mushrooms to the bowl.

2 Make a triple quantity of béchamel sauce.

3 Stir the fish mixture, with any juices, into the béchamel sauce and season with salt and pepper.

4 Layer the tomatoes, chervil, basil, fish mixture, and lasagna sheets in a large ovenproof dish, ending with a layer of the fish mixture. Sprinkle evenly with the grated Parmesan cheese. Bake in a preheated oven, 375°F/190°C, for 35 minutes, or until golden brown, then serve immediately.

baked tuna & ricotta rigatoni

ingredients

serves 4

1 lb/450 g dried rigatoni
4 oz/115 g sun-dried tomatoes in oil, drained and sliced

filling

7 oz/200 g canned flaked tuna, drained
8 oz/225 g/1 cup ricotta cheese

sauce

4 fl oz/125 ml/½ cup heavy cream
8 oz/225 g/2 cups freshly grated Parmesan cheese
salt and pepper

method

1. Lightly grease a large ovenproof dish with butter. Bring a large, heavy-bottom pan of lightly salted water to a boil. Add the rigatoni, return to a boil, and cook for 8–10 minutes, or until just tender but still firm to the bite. Drain the pasta and let stand until cool enough to handle.

2. Meanwhile, mix the tuna and ricotta cheese together in a bowl to form a soft paste. Spoon the mixture into a pastry bag and use to fill the rigatoni. Arrange the filled pasta tubes side by side in the prepared dish.

3. To make the sauce, mix the cream and Parmesan cheese together in a bowl and season with salt and pepper. Spoon the sauce over the rigatoni and top with the sun-dried tomatoes, arranged in a criss-cross pattern. Bake in a preheated oven, 400°F/200°C, for 20 minutes. Serve hot straight from the dish.

layered spaghetti with smoked salmon & shrimp

ingredients

serves 6

12 oz/350 g dried spaghetti
generous 4 tbsp butter, plus extra for greasing
béchamel sauce (see page 176)
7 oz/200 g smoked salmon, cut into strips
10 oz/280 g jumbo shrimp, cooked, shelled, and deveined
4 oz/115 g/1 cup freshly grated Parmesan cheese

method

1. Bring a large pan of lightly salted water to a boil. Add the pasta, return to a boil, and cook for 8–10 minutes, or until tender but still firm to the bite. Drain well, return to the pan, add 4 tablespoons of the butter, and toss well.
2. Make a double quantity of béchamel sauce.
3. Spoon half the spaghetti into a large, greased ovenproof dish, cover with the strips of smoked salmon, then top with the shrimp. Pour over half the béchamel sauce and sprinkle with half the Parmesan. Add the remaining spaghetti, cover with the remaining sauce, and sprinkle with the remaining Parmesan. Dice the remaining butter and dot it over the surface.
4. Bake in a preheated oven, 350°F/180°C, for 15 minutes, or until the top is golden brown. Serve immediately.

macaroni & cheese

ingredients

serves 4

8 oz/225 g macaroni
béchamel sauce (see page 176)
1 egg, beaten
4½ oz/125 g/1¼ cups sharp Cheddar cheese, grated
1 tbsp wholegrain mustard
2 tbsp chopped fresh chives
4 tomatoes, sliced
4½ oz/125 g/1¼ cups Red Leicester cheese, grated
2¼ oz/60 g/generous ½ cup blue cheese, grated
2 tbsp sunflower seeds
salt and pepper
snipped fresh chives, to garnish

method

1 Bring a large pan of lightly salted water to a boil and cook the macaroni for 8–10 minutes, or until just tender. Drain well and place in an ovenproof dish.

2 Make a double quantity of béchamel sauce.

3 Stir the beaten egg, Cheddar cheese, mustard, and chives into the béchamel sauce and season with salt and pepper. Spoon the mixture over the macaroni, making sure it is well covered. Top with a layer of the sliced tomatoes.

4 Sprinkle the Red Leicester cheese, blue cheese, and sunflower seeds over the top. Place on a cookie sheet and bake in a preheated oven, 375°F/190°C, for 25–30 minutes, or until bubbling and golden. Garnish with snipped fresh chives and serve at once.

double cheese macaroni

ingredients

serves 4

8 oz/225 g dried macaroni
9 oz/250 g ricotta cheese
1½ tbsp whole-grain mustard
3 tbsp snipped fresh chives, plus extra to garnish
1⅓ cups halved cherry tomatoes
⅔ cup drained and chopped sun-dried tomatoes in oil
butter or oil, for greasing
scant 1 cup grated Cheddar cheese
salt and pepper

method

1 Bring a saucepan of lightly salted water to a boil.

2 Add the pasta and cook for 10–12 minutes, or according to the package directions, until tender. Drain. Mix the ricotta with the mustard, chives, salt, and pepper.

3 Stir in the macaroni, cherry tomatoes, and sun-dried tomatoes. Grease a 7-cup ovenproof dish, spoon in the macaroni mixture, and sprinkle with the cheese. Bake in a preheated oven, 375°F/190°C, for 20 minutes, or until the top is golden.

vegetarian lasagna

ingredients

serves 4

béchamel sauce (see page 176)
olive oil, for brushing
2 eggplants, sliced
2 tbsp butter
1 garlic clove, finely chopped
4 zucchini, sliced
1 tbsp finely chopped fresh flat-leaf parsley
1 tbsp finely chopped fresh marjoram
8 oz/225 g mozzarella cheese, grated
20 fl oz/625 ml/2½ cups strained canned tomatoes
175 g/6 oz dried no-precook lasagna
2 oz/55 g/½ cup freshly grated Parmesan cheese
salt and pepper

method

1 Make a single quantity of béchamel sauce.

2 Brush a grill pan with olive oil and heat until smoking. Add half the eggplant slices and cook over medium heat for 8 minutes, or until golden brown all over. Remove from the grill pan and drain on paper towels. Repeat with the remaining eggplant slices.

3 Melt the butter in a skillet and add the garlic, zucchini, parsley, and marjoram. Cook over medium heat, stirring frequently, for 5 minutes, or until the zucchini are golden brown all over. Remove and let drain on paper towels.

4 Layer the eggplant, zucchini, mozzarella, strained tomatoes, and lasagna in an ovenproof dish brushed with olive oil, seasoning as you go and finishing with a layer of lasagna. Pour over the béchamel sauce, sprinkle with the Parmesan cheese and bake in a preheated oven, 400°F/200°C, for 30–40 minutes, or until golden brown. Serve at once.

mixed vegetable agnolotti

ingredients

serves 4

pasta dough

7 oz/200 g/1 cup all-purpose flour, plus extra for dusting
pinch of salt
2 eggs, lightly beaten
1 tbsp olive oil

filling

½ cup olive oil
1 red onion, chopped
3 garlic cloves, chopped
2 large eggplants, cut into chunks
3 large zucchini, cut into chunks
6 beefsteak tomatoes, peeled, seeded, and coarsely chopped
1 large green bell pepper, seeded and diced
1 large red bell pepper, seeded and diced
1 tbsp sun-dried tomato paste
1 tbsp shredded fresh basil
butter, for greasing
all-purpose flour, for dusting
3 oz/85 g/¾ cup freshly grated Parmesan cheese
salt and pepper
mixed salad greens, to serve

method

1 To make the pasta dough, sift the flour into a food processor. Add the salt, eggs, and olive oil and process until the dough begins to come together. Knead on a lightly floured counter until smooth. Cover and let rest for 30 minutes.

2 To make the filling, heat the olive oil in a large, heavy-bottom pan. Add the onion and garlic and cook over low heat, stirring occasionally, for 5 minutes, or until softened. Add the eggplant, zucchini, tomatoes, green and red bell peppers, sun-dried tomato paste, and basil. Season with salt and pepper, cover, and let simmer gently, stirring occasionally, for 20 minutes.

3 Lightly grease an ovenproof dish with butter. Roll out the pasta dough on a lightly floured counter and stamp out 3-inch/7.5-cm circles with a plain cutter. Place a spoonful of the vegetable filling on one side of each circle. Dampen the edges slightly and fold the pasta circles over, pressing together to seal.

4 Bring a large pan of lightly salted water to a boil. Add the agnolotti, in batches if necessary, return to a boil, and cook for 3–4 minutes. Remove with a slotted spoon, drain, and transfer to the dish. Sprinkle with the Parmesan cheese and bake in a preheated oven, 400°F/ 200°C, for 20 minutes. Serve with salad greens.

baked pasta with mushrooms

ingredients

serves 4

béchamel sauce (see page 176)
5 oz/140 g fontina cheese, thinly sliced
6 tbsp butter, plus extra for greasing
12 oz/350 g mixed wild mushrooms, sliced
12 oz/350 g dried tagliatelle
2 egg yolks
4 tbsp freshly grated romano cheese
salt and pepper
mixed salad greens, to serve

method

1 Make a double quantity of béchamel sauce. Stir the fontina cheese into the béchamel sauce and set aside.

2 Melt 2 tablespoons of the butter in a large pan. Add the mushrooms and cook over low heat, stirring occasionally, for 10 minutes.

3 Meanwhile, bring a large pan of lightly salted water to a boil. Add the pasta, return to a boil, and cook for 8–10 minutes, or until tender but still firm to the bite. Drain, return to the pan, and add the remaining butter, the egg yolks, and about one third of the sauce, then season with salt and pepper. Toss well to mix, then gently stir in the mushrooms.

4 Lightly grease a large, ovenproof dish with butter and spoon in the pasta mixture. Pour over the remaining sauce evenly and sprinkle with the grated romano cheese. Bake in a preheated oven, 400°F/200°C, for 15–20 minutes, or until golden brown. Serve immediately with mixed salad greens.

mushroom cannelloni

ingredients

serves 4

12 dried cannelloni tubes
2 tbsp butter
1 lb/450 g mixed wild mushrooms, finely chopped
1 garlic clove, finely chopped
3 oz/85 g/1½ cups fresh bread crumbs
5 fl oz/150 ml/⅔ cup milk
4 tbsp olive oil, plus extra for brushing
8 oz/225 g/1 cup ricotta cheese
6 tbsp freshly grated Parmesan cheese
2 tbsp pine nuts
2 tbsp slivered almonds
salt and pepper

tomato sauce

2 tbsp olive oil
1 onion, finely chopped
1 garlic clove, finely chopped
1 lb 12 oz/800 g canned chopped tomatoes
1 tbsp tomato paste
8 black olives, pitted and chopped
salt and pepper

method

1 Bring a large pan of lightly salted water to a boil. Add the cannelloni tubes, return to a boil, and cook for 8–10 minutes, or until tender but still firm to the bite. With a slotted spoon, transfer the tubes to a plate and pat dry.

2 Meanwhile, make the tomato sauce. Heat the olive oil in a skillet. Add the onion and garlic and cook over low heat for 5 minutes, or until softened. Add the tomatoes and their can juices, tomato paste, and olives and season with salt and pepper. Bring to a boil and cook for 3–4 minutes. Pour the sauce into an large ovenproof dish brushed with olive oil.

3 To make the filling, melt the butter in a heavy-bottom skillet. Add the mushrooms and garlic and cook over medium heat, stirring frequently, for 3–5 minutes, or until tender. Remove the skillet from the heat. Mix the bread crumbs, milk, and olive oil together in a large bowl, then stir in the ricotta, mushroom mixture, and 4 tablespoons of the Parmesan cheese. Season with salt and pepper.

4 Fill the cannelloni tubes with the mushroom mixture and place them in the dish. Brush with olive oil and sprinkle with the remaining Parmesan cheese, pine nuts, and almonds. Bake in a preheated oven, 375°F/190°C, for 25 minutes, or until golden.

cannelloni with spinach & ricotta

ingredients

serves 4

12 dried cannelloni tubes
butter, for greasing

filling

5 oz/140 g cooked lean ham, chopped
5 oz/140 g frozen spinach, thawed and drained
4 oz/115 g/½ cup ricotta cheese
1 egg
3 tbsp freshly grated romano cheese
pinch of freshly grated nutmeg
salt and pepper

cheese sauce

2 tbsp unsalted butter
1 oz/25 g all-purpose flour
20 fl oz/625 ml/2½ cups hot milk
3 oz/85 g/¾ cup freshly grated Gruyère cheese
salt and pepper

method

1 Bring a large pan of lightly salted water to a boil. Add the cannelloni tubes, return to a boil, and cook for 6–7 minutes, or until nearly tender. Drain and rinse under cold water. Spread out the tubes on a clean dish towel.

2 Process the ham, spinach, and ricotta in a food processor for a few seconds until combined. Add the egg and romano cheese and process again to a smooth paste. Transfer to a bowl and season with nutmeg, salt, and pepper.

3 Grease an ovenproof dish with butter. Spoon the filling into a pastry bag fitted with a ½-inch/1-cm tip. Carefully pipe the filling into the cannelloni tubes and place in the dish.

4 To make the cheese sauce, melt the butter in a pan. Add the flour and cook over low heat, stirring constantly, for 1 minute. Gradually stir in the hot milk then bring to a boil, stirring constantly. Simmer over the lowest possible heat, stirring frequently, for 10 minutes until thickened and smooth. Remove the pan from the heat, stir in the Gruyère cheese, and season with salt and pepper.

5 Spoon the cheese sauce over the filled cannelloni. Cover the dish with foil and bake in a preheated oven, 350°F/180°C, for 20–25 minutes. Serve immediately.